RAY FRENCH
...AND RUGBY

Ray French

RAY FRENCH
...AND RUGBY

Scratching Shed Publishing Ltd

First published by Scratching Shed Publishing Ltd in 2010
Registered in England & Wales No. 6588772.
Registered office:
47 Street Lane, Leeds, West Yorkshire. LS8 1AP

www.scratchingshedpublishing.co.uk

ISBN 978-0956252692

Unless stated otherwise, all photographs are from
the personal collection of Ray French

A catalogue record for this book is available from the British Library.

Typeset in Warnock Pro Semi Bold and Palatino

Printed and bound in the United Kingdom by
L.P.P.S.Ltd, Wellingborough, Northants, NN8 3PJ

To those who strive to attain for our game the nationwide
recognition and international profile it deserves

Acknowledgements

In attempting to record one's life in any sport the memory will invariably fail at the very moment one tries to recall the name of a player, the result of a match, an important career date or an incident in history. My experiences in writing this book proved to be no exception. So it was a huge relief to be able to turn for help when needed, via their many books and knowledge, to two of the St Helens RL club's outstanding historians, Alex Service and Denis Whittle, plus the Rugby Football League's own premier statistician, Ray Fletcher.

I am also greatly indebted to John Huxley and Graham Morris for their invaluable books – *Rugby League Challenge Cup* and *Destination Wembley, the history of the Rugby League Challenge Cup Final* – which confirmed a fact or two with regard to the influence on the sport of its most prestigious trophy - and my part in it, both on and off the pitch.

A checking of the occasional fact or opinion elsewhere has also aided me in presenting a fuller picture of the background to many of the arguments outlined, and I would like to acknowledge my debt to those authors and their books. The two volumes of Robert Gate's *Gone North* allowed me to testify to the deeds of many Welshmen, as did *Tries in the Valleys* by Peter Lush and Dave Farrar. The booklet *Code 13*, edited and published by Trevor Delaney, allowed me to confirm my thoughts on the development of rugby league's glorious past while uncovering an occasional gem of historical evidence. Many of my thoughts on the development of rugby union and its relationship on and off the pitch with rugby league were supported by my reading of the *Centenary History of the Rugby Football Union*, written by U.A. Titley and Ross McWhirter.

To all of the above authors I offer my gratitude for helping me to produce a book which I believe is unique, both because of my own experience and the advantage it takes of the scholarship of the past.

Contents

Ray French - The man behind the microphone

FOREWORD
by DAVID OXLEY, CBE
Former Secretary-General of the RFL
and Life Vice-President

I WAS delighted and honoured to be asked to provide the foreword for Ray French's latest book.

Dual code international player, coach, TV and radio commentator, author, columnist, after-dinner speaker, a proud and dedicated member of the British Lions Association – Ray is surely rugby's 'man for all seasons' (and reasons).

Like myself, Ray has always been an enthusiastic and totally committed believer that the rugby league code should constantly seek a national and international stage.

After all, if we truly believe it to be the greatest game of all, it clearly follows that we should strive to commend it to as many people as possible and in every corner of the planet.

Those who do not share this vision condemn rugby league to an eternity as a backyard sport. Yet, at the same time, it is they who complain most bitterly that their sport does not receive the media attention and investment it merits.

Folk cannot have it both ways. Make no mistake about it, a backyard mentality gets consigned to the insularity it deserves. Ray has always understood this and continues to fight most strenuously its perniciously belittling effects.

And finally, as he always says towards the end of his regular column in the newspaper *League Weekly*, I have been privileged to know Ray French for well over thirty years and to be able to call him my friend.

Throughout my term of office at RLHQ in Chapeltown Road, Leeds, he was always supportive, positive, helpful, wise and perceptive; his enthusiasm never flags.

He loves rugby league for its honesty, its humanity, its humour and revels in the skill, courage and essential modesty of all who play it, whatever their level.

These qualities, which he so exhibited and possesses in abundance, are richly celebrated in every page of this splendid book, which will delight, inspire and thought-provoke all who read it.

DAVID OXLEY, CBE
August 2010

INTRODUCTION

APOLOGIES to those readers who are expecting to read an autobiography, detailing every aspect of my involvement in both codes of rugby on and off the pitch. I have no intention of following the well worn path trodden by tabloid newspaper celebrities and 20-year-old sports stars whose egos far outrun the impact made by their lives. Instead, while naturally making extensive, detailed and often humorous reference to my sixty-plus years involvement in rugby as a spectator, player, coach, journalist and commentator, I hope to use whatever experience and knowledge my love affair with the oval ball has given me to consider the attractions, problems and the very future of rugby league and, to a lesser extent, rugby union.

I apologise too if my obsessive passion for league occasionally outweighs the evidence for my praise of its allure. But I make no apologies to those blinkered individuals who fail to come to terms with my liking for and also my enjoyment of the fifteen-a-side game. Whatever the effects on both codes occasioned by the breakaway of rugby league in 1895, I believe it is impossible to have a fair and balanced view of one game without having a similar outlook on the other. Hence I hope and believe that my activities in both for over six decades will enable me to better highlight the current strengths and weaknesses of my first love, the thirteen-man code.

The sight of me, aged eight, pinning a tatty piece of paper, ripped out from my Knowsley Road junior school notebook, onto our front garden gate and announcing the MacFarlane Avenue RL team would have led many to believe that I was destined for a career in league. That belief would surely have been confirmed whenever I, with a battered and torn old leather rugby ball under my arm, was seen leading all the seven, eight and nine-year-old lads of our local housing estate to Dodd Avenue Park, to play against the Ellison Drive Rangers. Or to the Congregational Church field for a match with a team from Hewitt Avenue.

If needed, further evidence of my infatuation with rugby league at a tender age could no doubt also be gleaned from the fact that I was the only boy on the estate who didn't possess a version of the craze of the era, a Subbuteo table football game. My Christmas present was a boxed set of the far less popular rugby version, which featured a novel plastic scrum complete with a hole in its top into which one dropped a small plastic oval ball before waiting for it to appear, almost magically, out of either of the holes placed at the ends.

Oh, the hours I spent flicking that tiny brown ball with my fingers into the hole in an effort to ensure that it emerged from the scrum to my set of plastic players. Hours spent chalking a miniature rugby pitch on the pavement outside our house, appropriately at number 13 MacFarlane Avenue, before inserting goalposts constructed out of a toy Meccano set and the playing of matchbox rugby were other signs that ballet was not to be my forte.

No formal autobiography then, but an account of how my life in rugby has shaped and formed my views on so many aspects of the handling game and given me the confidence to challenge some of the supporters with strong and, at times, controversial arguments about what's needed to take our sport forward. No matter whether there is agreement or disagreement with my opinions on both codes of rugby and their respective futures, I am sure that the inherently funny incidents and engaging characters to be met along the way will leave you content that rugby, whatever the intensity of our fervour generated, is still only a game.

1

A Boys Own Adventure

HOW could I ever forget my first visit to watch St Helens play at their Knowsley Road ground? Especially when, before half-time, I had captured two SS Panzer paratroopers and was forced to guard them inside a dilapidated concrete pill box situated at the back of the Kop End of the stadium. And, during the second half, had to shield them - and myself - from a hostile band of Apache braves, who just happened to be passing by, after buying sherbet lemons from a stall near the turnstiles.

Yes, my introduction to rugby league was exciting, even though our boyhood war games played out on the rough dirt banking then surrounding a large part of the ground took our attention off the real action on the pitch.

Indeed, for the first half dozen or more games of my spectating career, I can only ever remember looking grass-wards whenever there was a huge cheer which usually signalled that Saints had scored. Otherwise, I was fighting the Second World War with my mates well away from the goal posts or relieving a fort from a bunch of marauding Indians.

Such was the entertainment I received for my two pence entry to the Boys Pen, a railed off section of the ground behind the goal posts but one which failed miserably in its task of keeping all we youngsters confined in one place. Nevertheless, whatever the distractions away from the pitch, I and my friends could name every player in the then famous white jersey with the red band, could list every scorer and knew the exact score at any minute of a game. We were indoctrinated into the game at an early age, were enthusiastic for our rugby and passionate for a sport which has remained with me and shaped my life.

Oh, the names of the players who filled our heads with wonder and stirred our imaginations in those hard times immediately post War; men who provided me with the incentive and ambition to wear the club's famous, iconic colours many of whom were even to become my mentors in later life. How ironic it was that the very ones whose autographs I treasured in the late Forties should have such an influence on the development of my own rugby career and who implanted the seeds of the views and opinions on rugby league which I now hold so dear. And which, as I hope to show in this book, are still as relevant today - if not more so -for the good health and future of the game.

What talent deserted the rugby union clubs of South Wales to try their hand at the other code in the glass town of St Helens. In the Sixties, during the time of my own playing days at Knowsley Road, so many of their stars joined me in the pack that I seriously considered learning Welsh to communicate with the likes of John Mantle, John Warlow, Kel Coslett and Mervyn Hicks. But it was those Welshmen of the late Forties who kick-started Saints into becoming the famous club they are today and who were to have such a strong and positive influence on me. Players of the calibre of prolific try scorer and wing Steve Llewellyn, centres Don Gullick and Vivian Harrison, half-back Len Constance and forwards Reg Blakemore, George Parsons and Ray Cale helped the club in its task of stocking the trophy cabinet while two of them, surprisingly, were to play a part in me making two of the most important decisions of my life.

Viv Harrison, a stylish footballer who switched codes from the London Welsh RU club in 1950, came to teach English and help with the junior rugby at Cowley School in St Helens where I was a pupil. Imagine the excitement and sense of expectation that gripped me and another thirty 11-year-olds as we lined up outside the classroom waiting to have our first English lesson from one of our heroes. Once inside, I sat enthralled by all he had to say and willingly did all he asked. I never missed handing in a homework all year and not once did my attention stray when he outlined the difference between a noun and a pronoun or read from Robert Louis Stevenson's classic adventure story *Treasure Island*. Little wonder that, after studying the subject at Leeds University, I eventually became an English teacher for thirty-three years in both Widnes and St Helens, thirty of those years being spent at my own alma mater, Cowley School.

Steve Llewellyn, who had especially thrilled us all on the terraces at Knowsley Road whenever he performed his famous dive over the line for a try at the side of the corner flag, was to become one of the greatest influences on me when I came to making one of the biggest decisions of my life – whether or not I should switch codes from rugby union to rugby league. By sheer accident I met Steve one late July afternoon in 1960 in the small Sukey's Grill & Coffee Bar in the centre of town, less than a month before I finally signed professional for Saints and at a time when I was agonising daily over what I should do. We were the only two people in there and there was the usual embarrassing silence for a few minutes although we clearly both knew who each other were. That is until Steve, being the perfect gentleman that he was, quietly introduced himself and congratulated me on my performances for England rugby union that previous season. Then an assistant coach with the St Helens club, he raised the question of whether I was thinking of signing for Saints, Leeds or Oldham, the three clubs who had approached me about a switch of codes.

Steve's softly spoken manner and his courtesy and consideration for me that afternoon so captivated me that, although the only previous time I had spoken with him had been as a youngster asking him for a signature, I revealed everything to him and confessed all of my worries and concerns over becoming a professional rugby league player. Dwelling on his own union and league background and experiences on journeying from Wales, he eased my concerns and set my mind at rest. To his credit, he never advised me to sign for St Helens at the expense of any other club but spoke good sense about what should be my aims in life. After a couple of hours and another two or three cups of coffee, I left him and Sukey's Grill knowing that my mind was right for leaving St Helens rugby union club and accepting a tax free cheque for £5,000 from Mr Harry Cook, then the rugby league club chairman in the town.

Likewise, when I eventually put pen to paper, four of my childhood heroes had an equally big influence upon my on-field career.

Steve Llewellyn was the ideal man to offer me advice and show me what to do to make the transition from the unit skills and technicalities of union to the greater freedom of running and reliance on individual ability in the thirteen-a-side code. And it was another Welshman, ex-giant centre Don Gullick, whose advice and knowledge proved so useful to me when he and I were together as coach and captain with the Widnes club between 1969 and 1971.

The other pair who filled my head with ambition as a youngster and then, as coaches, guided me on my way through a rugby league career were St Helens' own former international stars, sidestepping winger Stan McCormick and Great Britain prop and skipper Alan Prescott. It was those twin personalities who were in charge of my formative years at Knowsley Road and who, aside from teaching me how to play the game, imbued in me to respect two fundamentals which have always been at the core of my attitudes to rugby, whether playing, coaching or watching it. I refer to my beliefs that rugby can, at times, be brutal but that the hardness of the game must be accepted and understood without complaint from a player or coach. And, while accepting that the arrival of full-time professionalism in both rugby league and union might have changed attitudes, that one should never take one's sport too seriously and that there is enjoyment and humour to be gained from it. From both Stan and Alan I picked up that while it was necessary to be totally focussed on a game and its outcome, regardless of my own personal circumstances, a sense of humour and a carefree attitude on and off the pitch would help to ease one's way through a long, hard, intense season.

Alan Prescott, who amazingly led Great Britain to success against Australia in a Test Match in Brisbane in 1958, despite playing for virtually all of the game suffering from a broken arm, taught me very early on in my league career how hard, not only physically but mentally, you had to be to succeed. Within a few weeks of signing for Saints, I played against a very powerful Swinton side at Station Road and, about fifteen minutes from the final whistle, had the misfortune to dislocate my shoulder. On moving close to the touchline and the trainer's bench on which Alan was sitting I mentioned quietly to him that I had dislocated my shoulder and was ready to leave the field. 'Which shoulder is it?' Alan asked. 'My left one,' I replied. 'Pack on the blind side of the scrum,' he advised. I did and had the shoulder pushed back into place in the dressing room after the game. Lesson learned!

Though Alan Prescott's successor as coach, Stan McCormick, took his rugby incredibly seriously and, indeed, worried alarmingly when results went against the team, he never lost his happy-go-lucky perspective on sport. So entertaining was he in creating a team spirit within his squad of players that he could easily have undertaken another career as a stand-up comedian. How I remember a trip one dark winter's night to play a fierce Hull team at their old, intimidating Boulevard stadium and recall Stan placing a large, old, battered brown suitcase on the team bus. Having refused to tell anyone why or what was in it, further mystery was aroused when he climbed off the bus carrying the object a mile or so from the ground while telling his players that he would catch up with them later in the dressing room. Thanks to the importance of the match and the intensity of the preparations for it, on Stan's return no one thought to mention his departure and the disappearance of the strange object. Until, on leaving for home after a fine win and with everyone in good spirits, Saints full-back Frank Barrow opened the bus door and climbed aboard. A scream from Frank and a frantic beating of his arms on the front seat alerted the rest of us to two or three lobsters running around the floor and crawling all over the seats while a dozen or so dead ones lay in the suitcase, the lid of which, to Stan's surprise, had sprung open during the match. After spending ten minutes catching the live lobsters and replacing them in situ, Stan at last confessed that he had called at the docks and bought the creatures to sell in his grocery shop the next day. That he did, aided by a large noticeboard placed on the pavement outside his shop stating: 'On Sale. Fresh lobster caught last night.'

It was not only my boyhood heroes who moulded my attitudes to rugby but some of the special matches at Knowsley Road, the visitors to the ground and the dramatic events surrounding the club which also captivated me and still lie behind my thoughts on the game today. My generation, whose schooldays started during the Second World War and finished in the Fifties, were fortunate that there were no televisions - at least for the first twelve years of my life, computer games, internet, mobile phones, iPods and other assorted technological gadgetry to distract us from playing all types of games and sport in the streets and fields close by our homes. Endless hours were spent playing cricket and rugby league on our local Congregational Church field with lads from the neighbourhood, many of whom went on to play club and county rugby union while others, like former Wigan and Great Britain captain Eric Ashton, gained fame in league. During the day, the only time the field was deserted was at 6.45pm when *Dick Barton*, a fifteen-minute daily serial thriller, was being aired on the radio, causing all to retire temporarily from the sporting action and dash home to listen while gulping down their tea at the same time. Normal service, of course, always resumed out on the field at seven.

Little wonder that the activities at Knowsley Road, standing barely half a mile from my house, should so concentrate our minds amid the austerity of those difficult but enjoyable years. The excitement and atmosphere of the special occasions there fired my lifelong enthusiasm for rugby league. The greatest sporting attraction and keenest anticipation in the town in that era was generated by the visits of the Australian touring sides of 1948 and 1952 when Saints, despite finishing in only eighth position in the league, beat the Kangaroos 10-8 in the first encounter and then convincingly put the tourists to the sword, 26-8, in the second meeting. The sight of those Green and Gold Aussie jerseys and the sheer size of the tanned, bronzed men inside them were the equivalent of invaders from Mars to us youngsters clinging to the rickety wooden fencing which surrounded the perimeter of the pitch. The programmes from those encounters were treasured and, when swapped among ourselves, were worth at least a dozen normal ones from any cherished collection. What tries! I well recall one sensational interception effort by Stan McCormick, the likes of which I have never since seen. When the Kangaroos' captain and full-back, the legendary Clive Churchill and winger Noel Pidding, were approaching the St Helens try line with only the diminutive Stan racing back to offer any resistance a visiting touchdown looked to be a certainty. That is until McCormick, running between the two Aussies and heading in the same direction, stretched out his arms, snatched the ball just when Churchill released it to Pidding, turned around and raced eighty yards to score at the other end of the field.

Such Kangaroo tours are now no more and neither are their counterpart trips Down Under, made once every four years by the British Rugby League Lions - but more of that later. No Challenge Cup replays now either to bind player, club and supporter together on a Tuesday or Wednesday afternoon and no opportunity today for anyone like me to miss his one and only day at school without a sickness note. But what a day that was. Wednesday 15th March, 1950 still confirms my belief that if rugby league is to capture the imagination of the public both locally and nationally, it must provide the circumstances to stage events which have a meaning and an interest beyond the normal fixture programme.

Having watched St Helens and Bradford Northern, as they were then known, play out a scoreless draw in a Challenge Cup round, I so much wanted to be a member of the 12,000 plus army of Saints supporters who journeyed by train, bus and car to Odsal Stadium on the following Wednesday afternoon to watch the replay. My only stumbling blocks were my dad, who was a stickler for discipline and a champion of my education and a stern headmistress at Knowsley Road Junior School. However, pleas from me and my mother finally persuaded my father to visit school and ask permission for my leave of absence to travel to the most eagerly awaited of games. An act of amazing generosity by Miss Henty allowed me to journey over the Pennines along with virtually the whole school population. Packed sandwiches, fruit cake, pies and bottles of dandelion and burdock pop were all loaded onto the fleet of buses and we kids were off for one of the best adventure days of our young lives. Until referee George Phillips blew his whistle at full-time before a 47,245 crowd and signalled an 11-0 win for Northern. But what an event, what a crowd, it created fans for life.

What an occasion too to stir the imagination in the August of that same year when a team from Turin in Italy visited Knowsley Road in an attempt to popularise the code back home in Italy - a country which, as I will later highlight, is now one of the many fledgling nations playing rugby league. To a ten-year-old boy used to hearing names like Lee, Harper, Jones and Morris being read out from the class register every morning, the visitors' line-up in the match programme indicating that Carnacchio, Francesconi, Tescari and the captain and former Italian RU skipper, Vincenzo Bertolotto were playing was romantic enough in itself. As was the exhibition match in the early Sixties between a team of American Gridiron footballers and a St Helens side including myself. It was hardly the forerunner of the current USA RL but, once again, an example of history showing the present what it can do for the future.

If ever a match in which I played at Knowsley Road indicates just what we have lost from the past that we must reinstate if we wish to secure a better future, it was the clash between Saints and an Other Nationalities XIII in celebration of the switching on of the first floodlights at the ground in 1965. Included in the St Helens squad were four Welshmen – Kel Coslett, John Warlow, Mervin Hicks and Ken Williams. Included in the Other Nationalities side were eight Welshmen including Berwyn Jones, Billy Boston and Stan Owen and four Scotsmen, Drew Broatch, Brian Shillinglaw, Rob Valentine and Ron Cowan. Oh yes, and in that St Helens team there were nine ex-rugby union players including South Africans Tom van Vollenhoven and Len Killeen, home-grown Keith Northey, Cliff Watson and myself.

As one grows older and, supposedly, wiser our memories can provide a comfort zone as a shield against the realities facing sport today and so it can be with rugby league. But I remain confident that my memories – and, indeed, experiences - as a spectator, player, coach, broadcaster and writer have enabled me to formulate ideas and opinions which are worthy of being taken notice of by those now actively involved in the organisation of the game at international, national and club level. To those passionate fans who I meet in large numbers on my travels around the country, who somehow believe that I possess supernatural powers of persuasion and urge me to sort out; refereeing problems, overseas recruitment, the standards of the England team or the rules in operation at the play the ball, I promise not to hold back from telling it as I see it, through my life in rugby.

2

French Lessons

THE 1944 Education Act, which introduced the concept of Grammar Schools and provided the eleven-plus examination for the brightest of our youngsters to gain entrance to them, indirectly achieved more for the development of rugby union - at the expense of rugby league - than any other factor since the original split between the two codes in 1895. Many such schools were created out of existing fee paying ones and, as newly created Grammars sought to imitate the model, values and ethics of the independents, virtually all encouraged rugby union as the winter sport for their pupils. Even in league strongholds like Widnes, Hull, Warrington, Wakefield and the like. So it was with my own Cowley School in St Helens, my home from home for seven years and a school at which I later taught for a further thirty. One to which I owe so much for its participation in preparing me for my life in both codes of the oval ball.

How proud and excited I was, in September 1951, to

walk to Cowley on the Friday of my first week clad in my new blazer and wearing a school cap. But of greater significance to me was the bag strapped to my back containing my rugby boots and kit for our first ever games lesson that afternoon. Rugby on the timetable! Almost two hours of it! What a pleasant prospect to end the week. But what a shock, especially for an eleven years old who did not even know that rugby union existed, nor had ever seen it played.

'How did you get on with the rugby this afternoon,' my grandfather asked me at teatime that night.'Did you enjoy it?

'I did,' I replied, 'but the teacher made us let go of the ball when we were tackled and nobody could keep it and play the ball. It was strange but I enjoyed it.'

'You are playing rugby union now, not rugby league. It's a totally different game. Don't worry, you'll get to like it,' he replied.

I did and still do but, after tea, I was in the field fifty yards from our house playing rugby league with my mates, little knowing that on that eventful Friday I was embarking on a life which would be enhanced and made all the more enjoyable by two codes of rugby, not one - and at times simultaneously.

Cowley School embraced all the characteristics of a typically good Grammar School in any northern town, a sound education, firm discipline and an indulgence in sport. Cricket, athletics, cross country running and many other individual sports have always been encouraged there but its forte has always been rugby and its renown throughout the country was made by its pupils' ability with an oval ball. Countless numbers of them have moved on to represent Lancashire RU and other counties, while some - Alan Ashcroft, Alan Brown, Richard Guest, Jack Heaton, John

Horton, Dave Carfoot and myself - have represented their country at rugby union. Others like Geoff Pimblett, James Roby and myself at St Helens, and Mick Burke of Widnes, have gained international honours at league. Unusually the school has achieved a reputation for fostering referees of distinction in both codes, with international arbiters Fred Howard and David Matthews in union and international whistler Norman Railton and Frank Tickle officiating in league. An impressive honours board but one which can not show the dedication of the staff to both games, their enthusiasm for rugby and, above all, the care and sympathetic attention given by them to hundreds of youngsters. One instance of such compassion and consideration shown to me in my first weeks at the Grammar school has remained with me over the past six decades and did so much to confirm my long held belief that any sport can teach so much out of the classroom.

It was another Friday, at 10.25am just three weeks into my first term at the secondary school and I was writing in an exercise book details of a small experiment just concluded by our physics master and junior rugby coach, 'Sparky' Watts. With my head filled with thoughts as to whether I would be selected to represent the school for the first time at rugby in the Bantams XV – a side including players of all ages who weighed under seven stones eight pounds – and waiting for the bell to ring to signal the beginning of morning break, I hardly noticed Mr Watts standing behind me. He leaned over my shoulder, placed a small piece of paper on my desk and said: 'Would you like to pack your books now and take this message for me to Mr Roddan before he rings the bell. And I would have a look on the noticeboard outside his room. You might be surprised at what you see.' Knowing that he had selected me to play my first ever game for the school in a team which rarely contained an 11-year-old, he wanted me to read my name on the team sheet alone without a mass of older boys questioning my inclusion. My heart beat faster as I stood there and read saw my name inked in and only in later life did I fathom out why the message for Mr Roddan proved to be a blank piece of paper.

I was launched on a rugby journey which has enabled me to visit countries as diverse as Papua New Guinea, Fiji, Uruguay, Australia, South Africa, New Zealand and many more and has allowed me to play with and against some of the greatest of players in the world.

It is my regard for both of the two rugby codes which has always led me to attack the bigots of one who seek to pour scorn or ridicule on the other and who fail to appreciate just what each has to offer participants or spectators. I have ever relished the chance to counter the abuse and criticism which has occasionally come my way for my enduring stance in both rugby camps. I take great pride and satisfaction in helping both Fairfield School in Widnes, where I initially taught for three years and Cowley School achieve considerable success in rugby. By introducing both league and union fixtures to both schools I attracted some concern in the respective towns and from some old pupils. At Fairfield, a secondary modern which developed a small sixth form, many talented lads were unable to represent their school on the playing field owing to the fact that rugby league competitions were then only held for boys up to the age of fifteen or sixteen years. Hence the introduction of an under-18s rugby union team, catering for the over age players and those boys who - though not able to cope with the demands or style of rugby league - could adapt their physiques or abilities to the other code.

At Cowley, after twenty years of coaching rugby union, I dramatically introduced league alongside, at all age levels, to a staunch fifteen-a-side establishment, again with huge success both on and off the pitch.

That success has, over the past forty years, been replicated in the universities and colleges where, after a friendly match between two groups of students at Leeds and Liverpool universities in 1967 and, three years later, the formation of the Universities and Colleges RL Association, the sport now prospers. Indeed, after once inviting invective from many union diehards at those seats of learning, rugby league is currently the dominant code at many. Half Blues are even awarded to students who take part in the annually televised Oxford versus Cambridge Varsity RL match. Since the mid-Seventies, rugby league has advanced massively among our students and how I enjoyed my time on a Wednesday afternoon, accompanied by one of league's leading photographers Gerald Webster, reporting on matches in Newcastle, Birmingham, Loughborough, Cardiff, Keele, Leeds, Nottingham and elsewhere for the weekly *Rugby Leaguer* newspaper. The introduction of rugby league to such places has not only provided folk like me with pleasure but it is now, along with other bastions of the establishment once out of bounds to the thirteen-a-side code, making inroads into the spheres of influence which rugby union has dominated for so long. That will help to take the game forward into a more receptive twenty-first century. The Independent Schools and Grammar Schools, the Armed Forces, the Civil Service and the Universities and the Colleges for over a century nurtured the union code and, whether deliberately or accidentally, played a considerable part in helping it maintain dominance over its rugby rival. It had the relevant ears and proved to be a major influence in the 'corridors of power', the media and the business world. Such an ascendancy might still be a reality but, in the words of the singer Bob Dylan, 'the times they are a changing,' for rugby league.

The Independent schools and, since the Second World War, Grammar schools have sent young men to the upper educational echelon where they naturally organised and played the game they had learned on the playing field – rugby union. It is also only natural that when such graduates eventually left their seats of learning for positions in Government, the Civil Service, industry, print and broadcasting - both at home and abroad - they continued to further the cause of their favoured game and play a direct part in its advancement nationally and internationally. Unlike the bulk of their counterparts in the northern towns of the likes of Wigan, Dewsbury, Halifax or Widnes who, having played rugby league at their local Secondary Modern, became a plumber, a machine operator, a coal miner or a council employee. Little chance for them to wield a direct influence as the Fifth Columnists could and still do for rugby union. Only in the 1940s, in Papua New Guinea where Australian soldiers, civil servants, bank employees and oil company workers in and around Port Moresby played rugby league in their free time were devotees ever able to exert a similar hold, enabling the locals to adopt the game of rugby league as their national sport.

Though the emergence of rugby union in Australia owes much to the students at Sydney University for forming a first club in 1864, in New Zealand to Sherborne School's Charles Munro who introduced the game to the town of Nelson in 1870 and in South Africa to Winchester College's Canon G. Ogilvie; the part played in development worldwide by the Forces cannot be overestimated. The crews of the Royal Navy played their part in arranging rugby union matches in whatever country they docked, the Army promoted it wherever its soldiers and especially its officers served and, in later years, the Royal Air Force joined them in helping to spread the game enjoyed by its crews.

But, why then, did no one in the three Armed Services ever attempt to recommend the game of rugby league after 1895 to any of the natives come upon by our brave soldiers, seamen and airmen? Because though a man could fight and die for his country he was not allowed to play rugby league for it. That is until - after intense lobbying in the House of Commons by David Hinchcliffe MP and the members of the All Party Parliamentary RL Group - the Minister for Defence, in 1994, finally relented and agreed to recognise rugby league and grant it the same privileges as other sports in all three branches of the Services. Today servicemen are representing their ships, units and regiments at rugby league and representative teams of the Army, the Royal Navy and the RAF are touring abroad and helping to spread word about their chosen code.

Ex-rugby league playing graduates too and even their universities are now underpinning the thirteen-a-side code and enhancing the strength and impact of the sport at both amateur and professional levels nationwide. Many universities and colleges now sponsor or act as partners with Super League clubs while others even support the Rugby Football League's most prestigious competitions. Leeds Rhinos is one club which has benefited from a major sponsorship with Leeds Metropolitan University and its Carnegie Faculty of Sport and Education. The club's players are able to further their education and prepare for life after rugby by enrolling as part time students at the university while the naming rights to the world famous Headingley ground are held by Carnegie. The world's most famous rugby league knockout competition, the 115-year-old Challenge Cup, is currently sponsored by Carnegie while one of the participants in the 2009 Wembley final, Huddersfield Giants, took to the field with the name of Huddersfield University emblazoned across the front of their jerseys.

The surge in interest in rugby league within such places and the expansion of fixtures between them nationwide is also now having a considerable effect on the playing side of the sport with ever increasing numbers of students and ex-students proving their ability and value in the professional arm of the game. In recent seasons, many have earned a place with various clubs in the Co-operative Championship leagues while students from Leeds Metropolitan and Leeds University helped out at Doncaster when the club was facing financial and player strength problems in 2009. Today there must be a huge smile on the face of Wigan-born Phil Melling, a lecturer at Swansea University, who in 1979 introduced rugby league to the Welsh students. While defying intense pressure both from within and outside the university to cease his activities, he soon became conscious that, for daring to offer a choice to some of his students to play rugby league rather than rugby union, his very job might be at stake. As he indicates: 'I remember being told I would get no further in my career at Swansea if I carried on with rugby league. I was taken aside and told that senior people in professorial and administrative positions in the college were saying I should stop straightaway. It may have been bluff but it was meant as a warning.'

No such open animosity and bigotry in the Welsh valleys today with universities, colleges, schools and amateur clubs enjoying rugby league and providing talent for the Crusaders Super League club and even the Wales national team itself. In the European Championship tournament of 2009 five Welsh Students – Rhys Griffiths, Lloyd White, Elliot Kear, Christiaan Roets and Lewis Mills – made their debuts for the winning full national side under the stewardship of former dual Welsh internationals, Iestyn Harris and Clive Griffiths. The impact now being made on the pitch in league at all levels by students and former students is highly significant, but it is off the pitch where the most important benefits can already be seen. Over the past twenty years or so, former playing students have made their way into positions of prominence in the world of business, finance, education, local and central government and the civil service. A few have become wealthy entrepreneurs. Many are now in the same positions of persuasion which were once virtually the sole provision of rugby union-favoured graduates and they too are now able to look kindly on any requests for help from the sport they so much enjoyed in their younger days. They too can channel the direction of a sponsorship or even a government grant and become a part of an 'old boys network', capable of giving generous consideration, whenever possible, to return the favour to the pastime that gave them so much.

No such residue of potential league players or code-friendly future businessmen from my seat of learning at Leeds University when I arrived to take up my studies in the September of 1958 but, throughout my four years there, I found a warmth towards rugby league from the students and the academic staff which I am sure was not then to be found at any other such establishment.

Large numbers of the students and some of the staff watched the Leeds RL club play at Headingley while others, who hailed from Wigan, Wakefield, Warrington and elsewhere, were the first to grab the newspapers in the university library on a Monday morning to read about their favourite team. The university invariably welcomed professional league players and during my stay the Leeds and former South African rugby union wing star Wilf Rosenberg studied dentristry. My good friend, the Wakefield Trinity and Great Britain full-back Gerry Round also studied there in the engineering department. I was invited to return to study for a Diploma of Education when I was refused entrance to Loughborough University when I signed for St Helens in August 1961. Such characters were highly respected around the university although, ironically, on one occasion Gerry's fame did not receive the acknowledgement it should have done. At the height of his prowess and after playing in a local charity game of rugby union under an assumed name, and having scored a hat-trick of spectacular tries, he was approached by a rugby league scout and informed that if he would agree to playing a trial with the Leigh club he might be able to earn a few pounds.

When I sat on a train at St Helens Shaw Street station bound for Leeds City and set to study English, Russian, Latin and History (what a combination for a rugby league second-rower) I confess that I had few thoughts in my head regarding the next four years of my education. Only rugby was on my mind. But little did I realise what opportunities Leeds University was to offer me for an involvement with both codes.

3

Union Dues

THAT I eventually ended up with an Honours Degree and a Diploma in Education after four years at Leeds University was a minor miracle such was the amount of rugby I played and the priority I gave to it. Indeed, in my final year in rugby union I played seventy-four matches of all types and importance including charity ones, guest appearances and club, county and international commitments for St Helens RU, Leeds University and the English Universities, Lancashire, the Barbarians and England. I trekked across the country for eight months with a kit bag containing a motley assortment of contents - rugby boots, socks, a towel, soap and copies of Virgil's *Aeneid* Book Four, P. S. Arden's *First Readings in Old English* or Geoffrey Chaucer's *Canterbury Tales*. Mastering the Anglo Saxon and the Latin texts on the train to the games proved far more difficult than the matches at the end of the line. But all ended happily in the end.

I was directed to Leeds University by my headmaster Walter Wright, a giant of a man and a former player at the university. I have ever been grateful to him for his insistence in making me cross the Pennines for if any university took its rugby seriously and played it to a very high standard it was Leeds. I consider myself fortunate to have played university rugby union at a time when the leading players at international and county levels still gave Varsity rugby their all and yet, being essentially amateur, they looked on it as a pastime and enjoyed themselves off the pitch as well. Standards were high and in my own university team were three England RU forwards in Bev Dovey, Dave Wrench and myself, a couple of English trialists and a host of county players. In the opposition ranks at Manchester, Durham, Aberystwyth and elsewhere were the likes of England, British Lions RU and future Great Britain RL stand-off star Bev Risman, England RU back-rower Derek Morgan and Wales RU centre John Dawes. The games were fiercely competitive and far removed from those now played at many universities and colleges where, thanks to the rampant and often self defeating professionalism of rugby union at all levels of the club structure, the absence of the better players is severely felt. Not so in university rugby league which, because the thirteen-a-side code rightly allows only one full-time elite league and two part-time professional ones at the top of hundreds of strictly amateur clubs nationwide, there has been a huge boost in playing numbers and strength.

Though I look back with pride on our victories over then leading clubs in the north of England like Headingley, Wakefield, Gosforth, Morley and others, and recall with affection some of the escapades I and my friends indulged in after the matches; it was when I was selected to play representative rugby union for the English Universities against the Irish, Scottish and Welsh equivalents that, especially in Wales, I learned very quickly what I needed to do to make progress in rugby union. In Swansea, Llanelli,

Maesteg, Ebbw Vale, Cardiff and tiny Blaina in the Valleys, surprisingly, I learned of an intensity of play and attitude on and off the pitch which indicated just what rugby league was to be when I eventually crossed the 'great divide'. And it was while playing and staying in those towns and cities that I first developed a tremendous affinity and respect for Welsh rugby, its players and its supporters, a respect which blossomed even more during my ten years as a professional rugby league player.

Talented Irish student backs of the calibre of Tom Kiernan, David Hewitt and Niall Brophy left a big impression on me whenever I played against them, but it was the club and international players of Wales who left the biggest impression - often literally - when I visited them on our annual Christmas and Easter tours. The crowds were vastly different in size and make up to the crowds I had been used to playing before in rugby union in England. The spectators in Wales were from the same social backgrounds as those who watched league in the north of England. They had the same passion and parochialism for their local club and they admired not only the individual running and handling skills of their favourites on the pitch but the ferocity, hardness and, at times, brutality which was evident for all to see. So did I suffer for my sport, not least on Boxing Day 1960 at the St Helens Ground, Swansea, while representing the English Universities against the local club.

Having already been selected in the squad to play for England against Wales at a sold-out Cardiff Arms Park three weeks later, you can imagine the reception waiting for me when I lined up in a student pack to face seasoned Welsh and Lions internationals like front-rowers Billy Williams and Norman Gale, back-rowers John Faull and John Leleu, and second-rower Idwal Fisher, who later enjoyed a fine career in rugby league.

From the attention given to me by the Swansea pack right from the kick-off and the urgings of an enthusiastic band of supporters full of Christmas cheer, it was obvious that I was to be the sacrificial English lamb. It was rough, it was tough and many were the amusing comments I received from the Swansea players, but when I left the field at both half-time and full-time the boos and the jeers which accompanied my departure confirmed that I had stood up to the test and not only held my ground but upset one or two who had assumed that baiting a seemingly naïve, young Englishman would be productive.

How grateful I was though to play in such matches and experience the fervour which surrounded them off the pitch, which was so akin to what I had been used to when watching my heroes play league. The previous reality for me at the time of my visit to the Principality that Christmas was a visit on a wet, damp Saturday afternoon to Rochdale rugby union club with my own St Helens to perform before a crowd of less than a hundred spectators, mostly half of whom were my mates.

County rugby union matches did attract considerable crowds and in the Northern Division the rivalry between Lancashire, Yorkshire, Cheshire, Cumberland and Westmorland, Durham and Northumbria was keen and healthy. There were many fine players who, in that environment, advanced their reputations and moved on to international fame. Such matches certainly aided my career and it is sad to see all the emphasis in rugby union in this country centred completely on the club game to the detriment of county representation. Great exponents from junior clubs joined the pathway to the top after selection for their county, not so today. Future northern international players of my era of the calibre of Alan Ashcroft, Malcolm Phillips, Sam Hodgson, Mike Weston, Phil Horrock-Taylor,

Bev Risman and others could showcase their abilities on at least half a dozen Saturdays early in a season. Equally, so could a number of lads like Barrow and Salford's Bill Burgess, Leigh's Tony Leadbetter and St Helens midfield duo, Peter Harvey and Keith Northey, who later played against and alongside me in rugby league.

But if there was one match which defined my rugby career and which heralded the start of a number of discreet rugby league scouts knocking at my front door it was the one played between the North West Counties and the visiting South African rugby union touring side at Maine Road, Manchester on Wednesday 23rd November, 1960. What a game and yet how different the preparation to today.

'Boks get a French fright!' was the headline on the match report in the *Daily Express* the following morning after our eleven points to nil defeat by the powerful Springboks. Though I earned extensive praise for my efforts over the exhausting 80 minutes play and the newspaper's rugby union correspondent Pat Marshall declared: 'England selectors have unearthed a real winner in Ray French, the big boy with the large appetite for hard work,' I don't think I frightened any South Africans. But, on reflection fifty years later, the thought of the team's preparations prior to such a prestigious match still does astound me.

The Springboks fielded a huge pack and, in their No. 8 Doug Hopwood and centre John Gainsford, they had two world class players who not only impressed me enormously with their athletic ability and ball handling skills but also Tom Mitchell, then the chairman of the Workington Town RL club, who promptly offered them record sums of money to switch codes. Sadly however for Cumbrian rugby league, both were content to remain in union. Despite the duo's abilities, the visitors only snatched victory in the final fifteen minutes of the match, but a clue to the reasons for their victory - and what today seems alarming - lay in Pat Marshall's match report.

He wrote: 'North West Counties' backs Bev Risman, Malcolm Phillips and Bill Petterson were streets ahead of their counterparts in the arts and graces of back play but they hardly ever saw the ball.' Little wonder, for given the total lack of pre-match preparation, the team could never hope to match the efficiency of the tourists. Having received my written invitation to play against them, the first time I ever met the rest of my team was when reporting to the ground in Manchester at 1.45pm, just forty-five minutes prior to kick-off. Indeed, it seems ludicrous that I should meet Mike Evans, the Wilmslow second-rower and my partner that afternoon in the pack, for the first time in my life in the dressing room and only have sufficient time to ask him on which side of the scrum he preferred to pack and in what position he wanted to stand in the line-outs. Hardly the preparations of the modern player who joins his team-mates in camp for at least a week before any game and is cosseted by a host of technical, scientific and coaching experts, all of whom tell him how to play and what to eat. Thankfully, my energy against the tourists was boosted on the train journey over the Pennines to the match by the consumption of two delicious pork pies bought earlier that morning from Leeds University's students' café.

I certainly would not advise a return to the primitive pre-match preparations of my playing days in rugby union but I do fear that, especially in the fifteen-man code, there is now far too much preparation and indoctrination which merely produces a set of players trained only to react as they have been told to any given situation on a field. Instinct, creativity and flair have been suppressed in rugby union's midfield in Britain. In the positions of those who once exhibited such talent, we mostly find capable journeymen who stick to a preordained plan and have been programmed out of offering the unexpected. Where are the stand-offs like England's Bev Risman, Richard Sharp, John Horton or Tom Brophy and Welsh maestros Barry John, David Watkins, Phil Bennett, Jonathan Davies and company; all of whom could offer a sidestep, a swerve, a sudden change of pace or a defence splitting pass to beat an opponent. Not from endless hours of training, they could provide an ingenious match winning moment from their own personal rugby repertoire.

No matter what little preparation I experienced before my meeting with the Springboks, my career in rugby union was now moving forward at a hectic pace while my future years in rugby league were already, unbeknown to myself, being planned by people I had never met. For, as the rugby league scribe in the *Daily Sketch* and an observer at the match Neville Haddock wrote: 'There were representatives from more than half of the rugby league clubs and in the crowd around me I saw officials from Wakefield Trinity and Wigan. The names rugby league fans ought to keep in their minds as possible future stars in the professional game are South African centres Alex Kirkpatrick and John Gainsford. Of the Counties, forward Ray French and Bev Risman really stood out.'

How Neville Haddock was to be proved right in his assessment of a rugby league scout's interest in Bev's and my attributes for, over the next dozen or more years, we trod together the same path through union and league. But first my immediate rugby career in union was highlighted by Pat Marshall, also in his match report, when he suggested that: 'Ray French will make a take-over bid in the first England trial for either David Marques' or John Currie's job.'

So it was on to Coventry and that first England trial and a way of life and friends, the likes of which I had never encountered in my first twenty years living in St Helens.

4

Sent to Coventry, England and Saints

THE new world into which my blossoming rugby career suddenly plunged me really did envelop me when, in early December 1960, I found myself in Coventry on the eve of an England 'Probables' against 'Possibles' trial match, confronted by a giant dish of lobster thermidor. The Hotel Leofric had welcomed me and another thirty or so players and reserves on the Friday afternoon prior to the match which was to be staged at Coventry Rugby Club's Coundon Road ground. My first impressions were that the hotel was certainly far more opulent than any boarding house I had been used to on my childhood holidays in Scarborough or Blackpool. But I never bargained for what proved to be my most difficult encounter of the weekend both on and off the pitch - my dilemma over how to tackle such a creature from the deep.

For twenty years my only contact with sea life had been a fish (battered cod) and split (mushy peas and chips) bought regularly from Alf's Chippy nestling in the lee of the

Saints' main grandstand on Knowsley Road. I doubt whether Alf himself had ever handled a lobster thermidor and never one like that, dressed with all the trimmings and staring up at me at dinner on the Friday night. Having gambled on which knife and fork to use I was confused over whether I should use the implements or my fingers to eat it. And as for which parts of the lobster I should attempt to eat, I was completely mystified until I delayed my introduction to the culinary arts of consuming such a delicacy by allowing a couple of my team-mates from the Harlequins club to start first.

I was genuinely surprised at the atmosphere surrounding the England trials system and the camaraderie among the players of both sides and the selectors in such luxurious and relaxing accommodation. It was somewhat similar to a top of the market holiday and the RFU hierarchy certainly intended the weekend to be enjoyed by all.

Though I only knew a handful of players from my Lancashire and English Universities squads, I found everyone to be so warm in their welcome and with such a generous spirit towards me. Indeed, whatever the differences between the two codes, I can honestly say that the companionship and friendships which I developed in rugby union and the hospitality directed towards me have always been, and still are, the equal of any I have found in rugby league. Sadly, though, on the pitch at Coundon Road both teams were greeted with thick mud, wind and rain and had to settle for a miserable no-score draw. Hardly the conditions in which to excel but the *Guardian*'s rugby union correspondent, David Frost, credited me in his match report with working 'extraordinarily hard and usefully' and the show moved on to Twickenham for the next and final trial between England and the Rest.

The protagonists and entourage all moved to a cosy hotel

on Richmond Hill in London, the team base for all England home matches at that time. But the atmosphere in and around the dining room and the lounges was far more competitive than at Coventry as the players realised that they were only eighty minutes away from winning an England cap. The England side contained some very experienced forwards, none more so than the long-serving second-row pairing of David Marques and John Currie, both of whom towered above me and were commanding in the line-outs. I and my second-row partner in the Rest XV, Coventry's John Price, would definitely have problems in that area and so it proved until I turned for advice some twenty minutes in to the game to a former pupil of my old school and very good friend Alan Ashcroft who, in the twilight of his international career, was the captain of the Rest XV.

Becoming somewhat concerned at the ease by which David Marques in particular was winning the ball at the line-out I asked Alan what to do as we were moving across the field to yet another line-out.

'Alan, I'm having trouble with David Marques. He's got four or five inches in height on me and such a good spring in his legs. Any suggestions,' I asked.

Alan, blessed with the experience and wisdom of sixteen England caps and a Lions tour of South Africa, hesitated as he followed me across the pitch and I noticed his brow creased in thought. With technical expertise and rare insight into my problem, he came up with the answer.

'Hit him Ray, when he next jumps.'

I did and things got better. Not only in the trial match for, despite an England win by 24 points to 5, I received yet another compliment for hard work - 'French worked very hard indeed to stem the flood' - from Peter Cranmer of the *Daily Telegraph*. Having been selected as reserve for the

England clash with South Africa, I was lucky enough to be drafted late into the team to make my international debut and play against Wales at the Arms Park, Cardiff on Saturday 21st January, 1961, when John Currie was forced to withdraw suffering from a bout of flu. The Marques/Currie second-row partnership had finally been broken after five years and twenty-two consecutive England appearances together and I was the culprit. The pressure on me was intense and I became the focus of media attention for twenty-four hours prior to kick-off, with one half of the newspaper scribes insisting that I was too young to be awarded a first outing and the other half backing my shock selection. In just over three months I had moved from playing for my comparatively lowly, local St Helens rugby union club to the England team. Yes, the pressure was on me but I revelled in it and couldn't wait for the kick-off.

Over fifty congratulatory telegrams arrived for me at our team hotel in Cardiff, from my club and county team-mates, former teachers and friends in St Helens and Leeds. I had never been the centre of such attention and, in the company of seasoned and famous internationals like England captain Dickie Jeeps, Peter Robbins, David Marques, Ron Jacobs, I was somewhat embarrassed.

A sea of mud and pools of standing water greeted both teams when we stepped on the Arms Park but such conditions didn't affect the commitment of both captains, Terry Davies of Wales and Jeeps, to playing open rugby whenever possible. Two tries from pacy home winger Dewi Bebb and one from England's wing flyer John Young down the flanks were an indication that the ball was moved around regardless of the soggy conditions underfoot. England's Bev Risman and Wales' Ken Richards both sidestepped their way through the mud and, occasionally, with clever changes of pace, sparked off many a backline movement to send the fans home happy, the Welsh supporters anyway, who enjoyed a slender 6-3 win.

I was happy too, though. According to the England selectors, I had acquitted myself well against a Welsh pack containing some tough and experienced forwards in hooker Billy Meredith, back-rowers Glyn Davidge and Haydn Morgan and big second-row Danny Harris, who later joined me in rugby league when he signed for the Leigh club alongside England's own cross-code convert Bev Risman.

It is worth noting for those rugby union aficionados who, over the past couple of seasons, have bemoaned the lack of exciting running and handling play in the fifteen-a-side code and the ever increasing incidence of goals at the expense of tries, that in the season in which I played my international rugby for England, the spectacle for the paying public must have been even more dour, despite the attacking qualities of many of the players. In my international season of 1960-61, England only scored twenty-two points (five tries) in five matches while their opponents only managed to grab five more. An even more startling statistic can be seen in 1958-59 when only twenty were scored by both sides in four England matches and not a try troubled the scoreboard operator.

Thanks to a different ruling then in use, the release of the ball at the tackle and the breakdown of play in my era of rugby union proved much faster and didn't involve the pile ups of bodies frequently seen today. A player could kick the ball from hand into touch on the full from anywhere in the field of play. Such a practice did limit the time for the scoring of tries and ensured that the high number of line-outs in a match restricted attacking opportunities for the backs.

For me, another three international weekends against Ireland, Scotland and France and the opportunity to enjoy myself on and off the pitch were looming on the horizon. But also, lurking at the back of my mind and always troubling me over the next six months, was the ever increasing presence and allure of rugby league.

The three remaining matches in the 1961 home international series proved to be excellent experiences and personally very successful. Though I received praise for my performances, I was especially delighted to play against those who possessed great ability and from whom I was able to learn so much. In their charismatic winger Tony O'Reilly, Ireland had a player to rank with the true greats of any era and it is little wonder that the major rugby league clubs yearned for his signature. In David Hewitt they also had a gifted centre to play alongside him and in Ronnie Dawson, Syd Millar and Noel Murphy, forwards powerful or quick enough to provide them with try scoring opportunities. Scotland, despite the vitality and enthusiasm of the pack only had their mercurial full-back Ken Scotland capable of carving through any gaps in our defence while a 5-5 draw with France indicated how close in ability the two sides were. The back row of skipper Moncla, Celaya and Crauste were blessed with such speed and ball handling skills that they were a constant threat to any side. With no coaches and the team tactics devised and led by the captain and the pack leader, it is obvious why international teams, for all the brilliance of certain individuals, then relied less on teamwork and more on the influence of one or two outstanding players for their success. In today's climate of programmed players, video analysis, month long training camps and a mass of skills coaches it does seem laughable to look back on a pre-match training routine for any rugby union international matches in the Sixties which, in an effort to sustain the amateur structure, insisted that no team could practise together more than forty-eight hours prior to kick-off. Hence the reason why, when playing at Twickenham, we only met up on a Friday afternoon at Rosslyn Park Rugby

Club's ground and practised for an hour on the first-team pitch before retiring to the clubhouse for a cup of tea, a biscuit and a team talk. Little wonder that such matches cultivated individual skills at the expense of any team preparation.

Weeks previous to my first appearance at the RFU's headquarters, I had been asked to contribute a pen portrait of myself for the match programmes and list any hobbies away from rugby. Watching rugby league and playing an occasional game of snooker in my neighbourhood Oddefellows Hall being my only two other interests at the time, I was naturally reluctant to place them in a Twickenham publication. Consequently I inserted skiing and squash as being my two other sports, even though I had never played squash and have still never strapped a pair of skis onto my feet. Imagine my horror when, at the Calcutta Cup dinner following the England v Scotland game, I was approached by one of the RFU committee who asked me where I did my skiing. Dumbstruck for an answer I replied 'Italy' and thought that was the end of the matter.

'I go to Italy,' he continued. 'Where do you ski in Italy?'

My mind was racing. I didn't know of any Italian ski resorts, never mind the name of one. And then a name did come to mind which at least sounded Italian, Burgi - the name which we, as young lads in St Helens, gave to the small mountain of broken glass waste which lay at the side of the world famous Pilkington Glass Works and down the slopes of which we slid on large pieces of wood or cardboard, often at the same time ripping the backsides out of our short trousers.

'Burgi, it's a small, quiet resort off the tourist track,' I answered.

'Oh, I must try there. I'll have a word with my travel agent,' he replied and offered to buy me a drink.

He wasn't the only person who offered to buy me a drink at the reception. Before I could even move off to take my seat the former Wales and Great Britain skipper, the legendary Gus Risman, approached me with a suggestion that he might come to see me when I returned to Leeds University with a view to my joining him at Oldham, then a powerful team where he was the coach. I had no hesitation in agreeing to his request and I realised that the time was coming ever closer when I would have to make a decision on my rugby future as other league clubs, notably Leeds and St Helens, were also showing a keen interest in my services.

Arthur Clues, the former famous Leeds and Australian second-row and a director of the Headingley club, was the owner of a sports shop situated just below the main entrance to the impressive Parkinson building which houses the main library of Leeds University. Being a wily, crafty character, Arthur, as an inducement to sign for his club, donated to me a new pair of soft leather, lightweight Australian rugby boots when I only called in to buy some new studs. How he ribbed me over the next ten years whenever I visited Headingley to play against Leeds for St Helens or Widnes and, always when in company, jokingly asked me for the five pounds I owed him for the cost of those boots.

Boots or no boots, it was Mr Harry Cook who, along with St Helens' current incumbent Eamonn McManus, was one of the most respected and influential chairmen ever to be at the helm at Knowsley Road, who finally persuaded me to switch my allegiance from union to league. He used all of his persuasive powers plus that aforementioned £5,000 cheque, a record at the time for any forward.

Though the headline in the *Daily Herald* on Monday morning 21st August, 1961 dramatically read, 'French joins St Helens - Saints officials clinch big deal at midnight', I actually put pen to paper for the chairman and the club secretary Basil

Lowe around teatime on the Sunday afternoon, after about three hours of discussion and cajoling. Why the need for further debate when, as a youngster growing up in a rugby league stronghold, I loved to play and watch the game and followed Saints avidly? Or when I was being handed a huge amount of money for merely signing a piece of paper which would allow me to do what I held so dear? Such questions might well be asked but there was much I needed to clear in my head before I was ready to leave St Helens rugby union club for the league one that bore the town's name.

Loyalty can be a much abused word but I have always been a great believer in the values of it, and it was mine to my friends and team-mates at the union club which troubled me deeply. A loyalty which has seen me return to Moss Lane, the picturesque home of the now Liverpool/St Helens rugby union club, to coach the team throughout the Seventies and to act as its president for the past ten years. I knew on that fateful Sunday night that my departure from rugby union would change my life but, unlike any player who decides to switch codes today between two fully professional games, I would be unable to return to play rugby union again should my venture fail.

The majority of cross-code manoeuvres have, since the professionalising of rugby union, been from league to union and any convert can still switch back to the original code of his choice if he fails to adapt to the new game. It was not so in the Sixties when any player switching from union to league was banned sine die from ever making a return. Should that player fail to adapt to his new code then a bleak future faced him rugby-wise and he could be finished as a player in his early twenties. I certainly didn't want such a situation to happen to me and that was my greatest fear, the possibility of not making the grade with the Saints and being left with no rugby to play. Silly but true.

The St Helens rugby league club, however, had great experience in the signing of rugby union players worldwide. It was an extraordinary intake of Welsh stars like Glyn Moses Steve Llewellyn, Don Gullick, Viv Harrison, Len Constance, Reg Blakemore, George Parsons and Ray Cale that, immediately after the Second World War, had helped to kick-start Saint's past sixty years of success. The signing of former Springbok union stars Tom van Vollenhoven, Len Killeen, Jan Prinsloo and Percy Landsberg - along with the extensive local talent on hand - underpinned the club's hunt for trophies in the late-Fifties and early-Sixties. In my own playing days, the signing of former fifteen-a-side men Cliff Watson, Ken Williams, Mervyn Hicks, John Warlow, Kel Coslett, John Mantle, together with local recruits Ken Large, Fred Leyland, Keith Northey and Peter Harvey, helped to stock the trophy cabinet with yet more silver cups.

Mr Cook had been or was to be directly involved in every one of those signings from rugby union. His experience in judging whether a player had the ability and attitude to make a success of any switch of codes was outstanding and unrivalled by any other club chairman, coach or scout. I backed his view that I would succeed in league and signed the paper he offered me from his armchair at the side of the fireplace in our house. I had travelled a long way from the days when, as a six-year-old supporter, I leaned or sat on that old, rickety, wooden fence which surrounded the Saints pitch. I now had high hopes I could do well from jumping over it to the other side and onto the pitch itself.

5

Welcome to League

WHATEVER the match, be it rugby union or rugby league, at Twickenham, the Arms Park, Landsdowne Road, Sydney Cricket Ground, Wembley Stadium or elsewhere, neither the opposition nor the venue ever held any fears for me. I rarely experienced nerves during my rugby career such was the confidence which I always had in myself when I prepared for a game. However I use the word 'rarely' deliberately for I must confess that, as I approached the St Helens first-team changing room door at Knowsley Road on the Tuesday training night following my signing for the club, I have never been as nervous in my life. No matter that I had represented my county, my country and the Barbarians, I was walking into the unknown and set to meet a group of players who, being the ultimate professionals, would judge me solely on my ability to master the arts of rugby league and my contribution to the future success of the team. Even more importantly, I would quickly be expected to contribute to the thickness of their wage packets.

I felt a sense of embarrassment and even of being somewhat of an impostor as I walked past the open door of the second-team changing room which, for the most part, contained a lot of locally-born lads who had risen through the schools and amateur club ranks and had received little more than fifty pounds for joining the club. Many glanced at me as they changed for training and I wondered what their attitude might be towards me; goodwill or jealousy. I quickly learned that their attitude would be formed essentially by my ability to prove whether or not I really could play the game, one which they then considered superior to rugby union. The pressures on me were mounting before I had even played a match in my new code.

In my era, any Welshman, Englishman, South African or Scottish former union player could try his hand at rugby league and, if he found himself lacking, could easily pocket his pay cheque and return home to his family and friends without too much worry. If I failed, I would have to live with that stigma among my friends and family in my home town, all of whom were fanatical league fans and rooting for my success in a Saints jersey. With professionalism in both spheres, there is now a safety net for the player who wishes to play both codes of rugby to a high level. For me, thanks to the draconian laws of rugby union then operating against being overtly paid, I would effectively be unable to play rugby anywhere should I not make the grade; a huge leap of faith for any 21-year-old lad to make. But I did have self-belief and, being a St Helens-born boy and a passionate follower of the sport, I did so much want to play rugby league.

I need not have been too concerned on that Tuesday night for I was welcomed warmly by all, especially by the local-born stars; Alex Murphy, Wilf Smith, Austin Rhodes, Brian McGinn and others. My boyhood hero, loose forward

Ray French ...And Rugby

Vince Karalius - known to all as the 'Wild Bull of the Pampas' for his devastation of the Australians during the 1958 RL Lions Tour - looked across as I opened the door and, sensing that I didn't know on which peg to hang my coat said: 'Come here, cocker. Get changed between Dick and myself.' Dick was none other than Great Britain second-rower, Dick Huddart, a giant of world rugby and one of the finest forwards ever to wear a Saints shirt. Suddenly there I was sitting between my two heroes and preparing to play alongside them in the back row of a Saints pack which contained two other Great Britain international players in hooker Bob Dagnall and prop Abe Terry. Cliff Watson, himself a former rugby union player, was to become one of league's finest international front-rowers within the next couple of years. Firstly, though, I had to contend with an 'A' team match against Swinton at Knowsley Road on the Saturday before I was to join them in the first team.

The club's coach, Alan Prescott, no doubt considering that I was too naïve to play against a good Swinton senior side at Station Road on my first outing, and the directors, without doubt hoping to retrieve some of my signing-on fee from my first professional appearance in the reserves being at home, decided that it would be better for me to gather eighty minutes' experience before tackling the big boys, Wakefield Trinity, four days later. Two home matches in three days, meaning two good pay days at the turnstiles for the club and a tough baptism for me.

My appearance in the 'A' team proved a most enjoyable first encounter with professional rugby league, taught me much that proved invaluable in my debut against Wakefield and, I think, earned me the respect of the lads who occupied the other dressing room. I was also made very much aware of the fierce aggression and, at times, brutality between players battling for physical and mental dominance which the more individually-centred game of rugby league encourages. In the opposition line-up was none other than former Welsh rugby union player Ron Morgan, a powerful, tough forward who, like me, was learning his trade with the second team before moving on to play a major part in Swinton's successes in the mid-Sixties. We clashed a few times and were both spoken to by the referee, all noted by the crowd and my team-mates who could at least see that I would have the heart and attitude needed to prosper. A try between the posts added further to my credibility with the local lads and, having won praise for my performance from our coach Stan McCormick, after the match I felt genuine warmth from my team-mates around me in the dressing room.

But the real test would come on the Wednesday night against one of the strongest teams in the league and a side containing some of the biggest names in the game, before a near 20,000 crowd. A majority were coming to weigh up the pros and cons of my abilities and to assess whether Mr Cook had made the right decision in tempting me to switch codes; everything to be judged in eighty minutes.

In international forwards Derek 'Rocky' Turner, Brian Briggs and Don Vines, Trinity possessed the steel and ball handling skills to launch their mercurial stand-off Harold Poynton and the England/South African centre combination of Neil Fox and Alan Skene to devastating effect. And I, regardless of my all-consuming interest in the thirteen-a-side code and playing of it as a boy in the fields nearby, was the novice of all the players who ran out of the tunnel and onto the pitch as the tune of 'Entry of the Gladiators' blasted out over the tannoy system. It was soon obvious, though, that in a game in which two players were sent off, Poynton and Saints' Austin Rhodes by referee Eric 'Sergeant Major' Clay, and which was described as, 'a shambles of countless cautions, crammed with unsavoury incidents', the signature tune was a most suitable accompaniment.

The music certainly highlighted the confrontation between me, the new kid on the block and Trinity's Great Britain second-row star and former Welsh union player Vines, ironically sold by Saints to Wakefield just one month before my arrival at Knowsley Road. Don, a strong running and tough customer, was intent on proving what a mistake his former club had made in their transfer dealings.

Within ten minutes of the kick-off, Don hit me with a ferocious tackle, ramming his shoulder just below my ribs and followed through with the whole weight of his body. I crashed down on my back, gasping for air and in intense pain. A loud 'ooooh' rose from the crowd, followed by cheers from the travelling Wakefield fans as all on the terraces and the players themselves realised that I had been felled by a magnificent tackle. The crowd waited in anticipation of what might happen next. Would Don Vines stand over a clearly stunned opponent who was unable to rise for the play the ball and look down at me like some boxing champion who has just dropped his rival to the canvas? Would the fallen ex-England RU player have to be helped to the touchline and out of the match on his debut to the accompaniment of a section of the fans crying: 'Not tough enough. Welcome to a man's game, Frenchie.'? Not if I could help it.

Though Don had hurt me, I knew that I had to haul myself off the floor to play the ball whatever the pain around my midriff. I had to make my rise from the ground appear as nonchalant and casual as I could and show no pain or concern with the challenge. I did just that as Don looked directly at me and said: 'Welcome to rugby league, lad.' It was a hell of an introduction but I was determined to return the compliment when I got the opportunity. That I did, about fifteen minutes later, to a similar outburst of gasps from the terraces and occasioned a smile from the genial Welshman when I said: 'Just returning the welcome.'

A ten points to five scoreline was a satisfactory win for Saints and, despite having to cope with many differences between the two codes, I was satisfied with my debut performance and more than happy to be among all the protagonists in the communal bath afterwards, to bathe amid the mutual respect and genuine welcoming spirit which the players have for each other in rugby league. Camaraderie exemplified when Trinity skipper 'Rocky' Turner handed me the soap and helped me to wash the cut above my eye which he had inflicted in a tackle. A spirit I also appreciated two weeks later playing against Hull when I stopped their captain and loose forward John Whiteley from scoring a match winning try seconds from time with a copybook cover tackle around the ankles. An exasperated John, having risen from the ground to hear the referee blow the final whistle, turned and told me: 'Ray, in rugby league, be careful where and when you tackle around the legs. Always try to use a smother tackle because if there had been anyone supporting me I would have passed the ball out of the tackle and we would have won.'

I did need to learn a thing or two about the playing style and tactics of rugby league, techniques which were often so simple yet proved to be so effective when one of them was explained to me by Saints hooker Bob Dagnall in our clash with Wakefield.

Throughout the period of my union career, it was the practice of the second rows on the break of the scrum to race off in the direction of the ball wherever it was on the pitch, catch up with the carrier by covering across the pitch and help to support any recycling of the ball. Instinctively, in the opening twenty minutes of the Trinity match, I did just that but, by the time I had covered across the pitch, the ball was invariably being switched back in another handling movement. As a consequence, I hardly touched the ball and was frustrated that I could not contribute as much as I had hoped. However, on attempting to race away from a scrum close to the touchline, I was suddenly stopped in full flight by our veteran rake Dagnall who grabbed my jersey from behind, tugged me backwards and said: 'Slow yourself down Ray. Stay here and the ball will come back to you.'

Within a few seconds it did return in my direction. I was able to make a break through Trinity's defensive line and learned lesson one of the differences between the union code and league in player alignment when in possession.

As I experienced, it can take up to twelve months for any player to master the intricacies of another rugby code and, though the laws governing rugby union in my era were far simpler at the breakdown and the scrum and there was far more space between the two teams whenever they lined up on attack against each other, rugby league still presented itself as a strange game to any newcomer from the rival code. There were some who spectacularly failed to adapt, whether because of size, attitude or a lack of ball handling skills, but the contribution to rugby league made by ex-union players, especially Welshmen, has been immense and must never be underestimated. Indeed, the game is in debt to many who have performed legendary feats and become record breakers following their cross-code conversion.

There are many within the thirteen-a-side game who appear to adopt the theory that a player must be born and bred in Lancashire, Yorkshire or Cumbria before he can become a true rugby league player. What rot! Any talented youngster can become a league player if he is taught how to adapt and history tells us that, once the barriers have been crossed, the former union player can gain the highest honours in league and make a huge contribution to the impact of the sport. Whatever their place of birth, many who have trekked north to try their hand at the rugby league code - or south as in the case of Scotland's Dave Valentine or Ron Cowan, and from across the Irish Sea like Ken Goodall, Paddy Reid, John Daly or Robin Thompson - have left their footprint on clubs as widespread as Huddersfield, Leeds, Workington, Halifax and Warrington.

The Oldham club has, in the past, welcomed ex-union forwards like Adrian Alexander and Sid Little from Harlequins RU club in London, while another stalwart of the Roughyeds' pack was 'Tug' Wilson who hailed from the Gloucester club. One of the club's most famous of players Alf Wood, who was among the injured heroes who battled bravely against all the odds to triumph over Australia in the famous Rorke's Drift Test in 1914 with a team reduced to ten men, was born in Wolverhampton. The Salford club welcomed two English players from Harlequins and Moseley in Tom Danby and Keith Fielding, both of whom represented Great Britain RL. And few former union players ever made as big an impact as my team-mate at St Helens, prop-forward Cliff Watson, who made three trips Down Under with the British Lions RL squad. He was born within the sound of Bow Bells in London and reared in the Midlands with the Dudley Kingswinford club. Oh yes, and what of wing flyer Martin Offiah, once an unknown at Rosslyn Park, who was signed by Widnes coach Doug Laughton and grabbed over 500 tries in a career in league?

No country, however - despite the influx of an amazing array of talent from South Africa in the Fifties and Sixties in the likes Tom van Vollenhoven, Jan Prinsloo, Len Killeen, Wilf Rosenberg, Gert Coetzer, Alan Skene and company - has ever contributed as much as Wales. There the union code, until the mid-Nineties, has been a production line for some of the greatest names in rugby league. The names of icons Jim Sullivan, Gus Risman, Lewis Jones and Billy Boston are revered in the sport. The record books of many clubs highlight the try or goal scoring feats of such as Billy Boston, Johnny Ring and Jim Sullivan (Wigan); Kel Coslett and Steve Llewellyn (St Helens); Gus Risman, Maurice Richards and David Watkins (Salford); Lewis Jones (Leeds) and are ample evidence of the code's debt to the men from the Valleys. Seven Welshmen took part in the first ever Lions RL tour of the Southern Hemisphere in 1910, while in 1946, under the captaincy of Wales and Salford's Gus Risman, a record eleven Welshmen travelled with the tourists to Australia and New Zealand. Leaving aside the 1920s to the 1950s when union players by the bus load left the Principality, between 1970 and 1990 over thirty-three international union stars from all over Britain, including Alan Tait, Tommy David, John Bentley, Jonathan Davies, John Devereux, David Bishop and Glyn Shaw, switched codes.

No such numbers of talented union players are currently coming to join the professional ranks of rugby league and, at both club and international level, our game is feeling the loss more than many realise. Thanks to the professionalising of union and the size of salaries being handed to the code's leading stars, there is no real enthusiasm for a switch from union and because of the implications of the annual salary cap on players' wages in league, there is no rush to welcome converts by the club coaches. It is a misguided policy and I believe that it is time the clubs looked once more at the latent talent on show in union and took steps to merge it with the outstanding league ability developed nearer home.

There is much merit in the idea of having any union convert's wages and payments taken off the salary cap restrictions, a procedure which would allow any coach to take a gamble with a player without penalising the strength of a club's squad and/or reducing the finances available should the player fail to adapt to the demands of league. When at Wigan, former coach Brian Noble was a staunch supporter of such a system and did indicate to me that he knew of union players who would have been prepared to switch codes, however temporary, if it had been sanctioned by the Rugby Football League and the Super League clubs.

Not only are there British rugby union players out there who might be willing to sample the delights of rugby league, we would do well to visit the Pacific Islands and, as St Helens once did from Samoa, seek out the next Apollo Perelini or Maurie Fa'asavalu. League needs to increase its player base if it is ever to challenge the might of Australia for world domination and make itself more attractive to a nationwide audience.

But, back to the rugby league career which confronted me at a time when no such problems troubled our club scouts and the international selectors; to an era when league players were unable to cross the once 'great divide' not only to play rugby union but also to coach the game. A far cry from headlines in recent years announcing such as, 'Wigan's Andy Farrell to join Wasps RU Club' or 'League's Phil Larder to help coach England RU'.

6

Learning the Ropes

REGARDLESS of the current attractions of both codes of rugby, the legislators of the two games have grappled for over a century with the problem of how to bring the ball back into play following a tackle. As early as 1906 the Rugby Football League - or more accurately Northern Union as it was then known - introduced a play the ball which required the tackled player to rise immediately and tap the ball in any direction with his foot, and usually to a team-mate. With often less than a yard between the teams such a system failed to allow any build up and continuity until the tackled player was instructed to bring the ball back into play to his own side by tapping it with his foot between his legs - a format which allowed a team to retain possession for an unlimited period until an infringement and a scrum was then formed. A four tackle rule, following trials in BBC TV's Floodlit Trophy competition, was introduced in 1966 whereby a scrum was to be formed after four consecutive tackles unless the attacking side kicked the ball or lost possession. A raise in the number of tackles to six in 1972 and, eventually, after five, the handing over of the ball to the defending side if no kick is made, has now become the ultimate compromise which appears to satisfy most rugby league devotees.

As one who has played or watched rugby league under all varieties - and even one tackle rules, more of that farcical match later - the various regulations concerning such a fundamental aspect of the game have dramatically altered the style, tactics and demands on the individual players. Likewise, the differing modes of play have constantly altered the attractions of the sport for its supporters and even determined the success - or otherwise - of its clubs, as they sought to come to terms with such changes. It was certainly so during my playing career with St Helens.

But firstly let me debunk a theory which still carries some credence with many of the older fans of rugby league and some historians, that the eras of the unlimited tackle rule provided endless, monotonous forward charges around the play the ball and a creeping barrage mentality from teams determined to avoid defeat by retaining possession for as long as they could.

It was such an outlook that led to the unique match played under a one tackle rule between a Great Britain XIII and a French equivalent at Parc Des Princes Stadium in Paris in October 1961, devised by the then secretary of the RFL, Bill Fallowfield, a former union and amateur league player. The match, involving almost exclusively players from an ex-union background like Bev Risman, Charlie Renilson, Danny Harris, Tom van Vollenhoven, Colin Greenwood, Alan Skene and myself was a disaster. It turned out to be a complete farce of a match as both sets of players scrambled and scrapped frantically for the ball on the ground and then threw it anywhere across the pitch to avoid another tackle. By half-time, all the players were so tired that the final forty minutes became akin to walking touch rugby. Little wonder that Mr Fallowfield, though a staunch advocate of the eventual introduction of the four and six tackle rules, abandoned his experiment before returning with a bemused GB team from across the Channel.

Although I believe that the limitations placed on the number of tackles able to be absorbed by an attacking side has proved to be a success and is, in part, responsible for the vibrant, running and handling spectacle that modern rugby league now is, I also think that the game lost much in the arts of wing and forward play which were so evident in mine and previous playing eras. If, as the myths would have it, teams in days of yore plodded downfield with the ball 'stuffed up their jerseys' and gained a win by merely denying the opposition possession, how is it that some of the greatest heroes in the sport are wingers from the earlier eras who scored an amazing number of tries per season? And how is it that their counterparts in the forwards are renowned not for their barging, plodding tactics but for their superior ball handling skills and an often uncanny ability to pass the ball out of the tackle, thereby creating a try or a free flowing handling movement?

Where, today, under the current rules, are the wingers of genuine pace, possessing a swerve or side step to challenge the likes of Brian Bevan, Billy Boston, Tom van Vollenhoven, Mick Sullivan, Lionel Cooper, Jack McLean, Brian Nordgren and company who registered upwards of fifty, sixty or seventy-plus touchdowns per season? And where are the forwards who can rival Vince Karalius, Brian McTigue, Johnny Whiteley, John Tembey, Johnny Ward and others with their subtle ball handling techniques? Despite Bill Fallowfield and his disciples' constant call for change in the early Sixties, there was little on the horizon for at least five years to stop me from first learning my trade with St Helens and then enjoying what I had always wanted to do, play professional rugby league - under any kind of rules.

It was soon obvious to me that the first Saints pack in which I became a part, thanks to the sheer power, physical prowess and the ideal mix of its members, was perfectly suited to the demands of the unlimited tackle rule. And, in an era when great care was taken in the composition of the six forwards, it was not unexpected when, in October and November of '61, we beat first the touring New Zealand side 25-10 and then won the Lancashire Cup Final, defeating Swinton equally convincingly, 25-9.

The front row was expected to consist of a clever, ball playing open-side prop, a hooker who could guarantee possession from the majority of the scrums and dictate play from the acting-half-back position and another tough tackling bulwark who could charge out of defence and make inroads into the opposition's ranks. In Abe Terry, Bob Dagnall and Cliff Watson, we had just that combination. The back-row trio was invariably made up of one strong running second-rower who could pick up tries out wide by virtue of his pace and power and a partner who put in a heavy tackling stint, as well as carrying out the donkey work in midfield. I started life at Knowsley Road as the donkey to Dick Huddart, one of the fastest and most prolific of try scorers ever to play in a Saints or Great Britain pack. In the number thirteen jersey, it was customary to install a clever but tough ball playing loose forward who could direct play, link with both the forwards and the backs and provide a last line of cover in defence. Our skipper, Vince Karalius, the scourge of the Aussies, was acknowledged worldwide as being supreme in that position and, though I only played alongside him for a short period - before he was transferred at his own request to Widnes, I learned so much from him.

He especially taught me the need to build up my physical strength to combat the ferocity of the one-on-one tackles and to be able to break through the tightest of defences in midfield. Vince was the first person to suggest to me the need to indulge in some weight training, then an exercise almost unknown in any club's training regime and far removed from the intensity of the exercises performed, almost obsessively, in a specialist gymnasium by modern players. In the current full-time era, players can pursue weights every day and add to their natural strength, but in the part-time world, when training consisted of two nights per week and Monday to Friday saw me active as a schoolteacher, there were few opportunities to bulk myself up or add power to my legs and upper body.

Being a miner, drayman and a scrap metal merchant respectively, Dick Huddart, Cliff Watson and Vince Karalius were heaving, lifting and dragging coal, beer barrels or scrap while I was writing on a blackboard with a piece of chalk. They hardly needed weight training such was their physical development, but I was so grateful when Vince, whose strength was such that I always imagined him as walking around at work with two steel girders under each arm and with a zinc bath balanced on his head, made a primitive set of weights for my personal use. My regular sessions on them did help me to withstand the greater intensity and the sheer physicality of league while the more matches I played in, the more I became acquainted with what I needed to do to become a regular in the Saints pack.

Unfortunately, though I did make progress and, during my first couple of seasons in the famous red and white jersey various cups found their way into the club's trophy cabinet, the period proved to be the break up of a once great side which had won the Challenge Cup four months before my arrival. But it also saw the rebuilding of a team that was to bring even more honours to the town. During my first three years at Knowsley Road, under the coaching of firstly Alan Prescott and then, following his dismissal in January 1962, under the stewardship of Stan McCormick, there was never a settled side which could mould itself together. But whatever problems the arrivals and departures caused for Alan and Stan, the core of the team which was to sweep all before it in the mid-Sixties was deliberately or accidentally being formed by a board of directors who were ruthless in their search for success.

The 1961 Wembley heroes Vince Karalius, Dick Huddart, Abe Terry, Don Vines, Mick Sullivan, Brian McGinn, Austin Rhodes and Ken Large all left for pastures new, while one of my second-row partners and then one of the most exciting runners in the game, Jim Measures, was surprisingly transferred to Widnes. Although quality ball playing forwards like Bill Major, John Tembey and Welshman Stan Owen, were signed from Widnes, Whitehaven and Leigh, it was the ever increasing number of ex-rugby union players, allied to the swelling ranks of the highly talented locals which, according to the record keepers, eventually created a team to rank with any in the St Helens club's history. From Wales came prolific points scorer Kel Coslett, classy centre Ken Williams and powerful forwards John Warlow and John Mantle. South Africa provided Len Killeen, a winger who bagged tries and goals whenever he played, and from nearer home came St Helens-born Tom Pimblett, an England RU wing trialist and Peter Harvey, a clever stand-off who invariably helped himself to twenty tries a season courtesy of his eye for a gap and shrewd support play. Alongside those converts, youngsters Billy Benyon, Frank and Tony Barrow, Doug Laughton and others developed into the outstanding talents they eventually became at St Helens and elsewhere.

Dislocation to a settled team there might have been and we might have failed to lift the First Division Championship trophy, but there were still a couple of Lancashire Cup Finals to savour with wins against Leigh and Swinton and a particularly eventful match in May 1964 for myself and my good friend Stan McCormick in the Western Division Championship decider, a tournament which had replaced the old Lancashire League competition.

Seemingly as ever, our major rivals and the First Division champions of 1963/64 Swinton, were the opposition and, having been defeated in so many finals by St Helens, the pressure really was on the Lions to win this match played before a 17,363 crowd at Central Park, Wigan. It did appear that they were finally going to get the better of us when, having trailed by seven points at half-time thanks to a Keith Northey try and two Kel Coslett goals, they roared back to parity with a try from winger John Stopford and two goals from their wily skipper Albert Blan. With less than five minutes remaining it appeared that Saints were a spent force and that our deadly rivals were getting the upper hand. That is until Alex Murphy darted past a tiring Lions defender and slipped the ball to John Warlow, who continued the movement before passing to our deceptively pacy prop John Tembey.

John, who had been bought to fill the place vacated by Abe Terry and to provide the team with some of his perfectly timed, defence breaking passes, provided me with one of his finest efforts and the opportunity to race fifteen yards to the line for the winning try. Handshakes, back slapping and smiles all around followed and there was huge personal satisfaction, not just for scoring the try which clinched the result but because, as any rugby league statistician will tell you, tries from Ray French in a Saints jersey were rarer than sighting a cuckoo in January. That touchdown helped me on my way to achieving a ten try haul from 201 appearances for the Saints. Hardly the stuff of legends, but I was all smiles as I made my way to receive my winners medal and to shake hands and have a chat with our coach. Yet Stan, who I expected to have rushed onto the pitch at the final whistle such was his enthusiasm, was nowhere to be seen. Until, suddenly, a large group of supporters on the touchline parted and four stretcher bearers emerged carrying our forlorn supremo, his face and shirt covered in blood and with a huge bandage wound around his head.

Though a sad sight to behold, I and my team-mates burst into uncontrolled laughter when, after asking what had happened to him, Stan replied: 'It's your bloody fault. When you scored that try I was so surprised I jumped up and hit my head on the concrete roof. I'll miss the presentation ceremony now. I've got to have the cut stitched in the dressing room.' Twelve stitches and a headache, but at least he had seen his team win the Cup. Not that our success did Stan any good for, within a week, he had been sacked and in most humiliating circumstances - while returning home on the team bus after our last match of the season at Castleford. Incredible as it may seem Stan, who was in high spirits and singing with the players on the back seat of the bus, was called to the front where the directors were sitting and told that he no longer had a job. Such a brutal and cruel decision was typical of the Saints management at the time and one which indicated the single mindedness of the chairman Mr Cook, in his constant pursuit of yet more trophies. It was that desire which led him and his board of directors to sanction what was - and probably still is - one of the biggest gambles in the history of the St Helens club, the naming of Joe Coan as the next in charge.

Eyebrows were raised before the beginning of the 2010 Super League season when Michael Maguire, the assistant coach at Melbourne Storm, was selected as the Wigan Warriors' head man to replace Brian Noble. No one doubted Michael's credentials but some fans did ask Wigan chairman Ian Lenegan why an assistant coach from another club had been appointed to take charge of one of the most famous rugby league clubs in the world. Imagine the wonderment and the surprise then when, before the beginning of the 1964/65 season, a man who had never played or coached rugby league was appointed to take charge of a St Helens team which contained some of the greatest players in the world. That man, a schoolmaster at the local West Park Grammar School in town, but a complete unknown in the world of rugby league, was Joe Coan. Though barely older than the players, he was to prove that Mr Cook's judgement was no gamble, for over the next four years he helped the club to reap huge dividends.

Joe, a PE teacher, had first made his presence felt during the 'great freeze' of 1962/63 when, because of the cold weather, Saints played no matches for almost three months and he was called in to help Stan McCormick with the players' physical training in a local school gymnasium. For nearly three months, two nights per week, Joe introduced us to some stiff indoor fitness regimes and soon gained our respect and a reputation among the club's board members for his discipline and dedication. A lack of knowledge and experience of rugby league on his part didn't trouble them when they made their controversial decision to replace Stan McCormick with a complete novice.

Today, when coaches have to gain all the levels of certificates and have to put time in at amateur, academy and assistant posts before they can even consider applying for a head coach's role, no club would ever contemplate appointing a man so lacking in qualifications as Joe Coan. Any such suggestion would be laughed out of the boardroom and have scorn and ridicule heaped upon it by the club's supporters. A glance at the line-up of engage Super League coaches at the beginning of the 2010 season - nine overseas to five English - indicates that an Australian or a Kiwi is invariably favourite to land the top coaching jobs in this country. And before he can obtain a visa to leave the Southern Hemisphere for a stint in Europe he too must have all the necessary paper and practical qualifications.

Have we built up too much of a mystique and aura around our leading coaches and do we overestimate just what many of them can produce? Are we too obsessed with employing a rugby guru whose scientific theory and over indulgence in technology and tactics actually hinders the natural development of the individual player and the team as a whole? Has the huge influx of highly qualified coaches from Australia and New Zealand actually done much to raise our standards to such an extent that we can at last challenge those countries for world domination in rugby league? It would hardly seem so. Was it their superior knowledge and techniques which allowed former Kiwi and Aussie coaching maestros Graham Lowe and John Monie to win so many trophies for the invincible Wigan teams between 1986 and 1993? Or was it more their personal qualities and man management allied to the extraordinary strength of a squad containing many of the greats of rugby league like Joe Lydon, Dean Bell, Andy Gregory, Shaun Edwards, Ellery Hanley, Denis Betts, Andy Platt, Andy Farrell, Gene Miles, Martin Offiah, Phil Clarke, Jason Robinson, Bobbie Goulding, Kevin Iro, Andy Goodway and so many more?

Joe Coan possessed no rugby league coaching qualifications whatsoever and had never donned a jersey to play the sport, yet he knew all that was necessary to get a man fit to play the game. The Cumbrian schoolteacher was intelligent and articulate, able to maintain a firm discipline over his charges by virtue of mutual respect and had a patient understanding of the needs and demands of the players. He was a good organiser and a manager. He acknowledged and encouraged the players' superior rugby knowledge and he possessed a sense of humour which often aided team spirit. Like Graham Lowe and John Monie, he was the right man to be placed in charge of a team which, like the great Wigan team of the Eighties, had an abundance of the stars of the Sixties.

7

The Toughest of Springboards

DURING his first two full seasons in charge, between1964 and 1966, Joe Coan certainly had under his control a squad of players that was the envy of any other coach in the game. Obviously realising that his knowledge of rugby league then was far inferior to the players, he concentrated on the two aspects which were to be central to his coaching beliefs – discipline and fitness. Such was the quality of the many international stars then playing at Knowsley Road, the outstanding promise of the rugby union converts and the ability of the locals from the amateur ranks, under the captaincy of Alex Murphy, he could virtually allow them to shape the style of play and tactics themselves. Given the many and varied skills of the individuals in the side and also their physical and mental toughness, Joe was shrewd enough to realise that, under the unlimited tackle rule, if his team was far superior in fitness to any other in the league, then his side would invariably win most contests in the final twenty minutes of a match. Having suffered under his training regimes for three years, I can honestly say that, in any part-time era, I cannot believe that I could have improved upon my physical prowess. I and my team-mates were probably in the best shape and condition of our playing careers during our days spent under Joe and, given the variety and mix of talent available to him, it is little wonder that the club's trophy cabinet bulged.

When building a successful team, the coach needs to pay as much attention to the blend, character and make up of his charges as to their individual skills. His board of directors often need to be bold and take a gamble when signing a player. They need to be prepared to sign the best whatever the cost and to attract recruits from the most unexpected of places - as well as never forgetting to nurture the local amateur league and union talent. St Helens did just that and profited on and off the pitch with a side that possessed the ideal, which also contributed to the good health of the national team's prospects.

Under Coan, St Helens' trophy winning sides were populated by many outstanding players but the greatest of them all was mercurial scrum-half Alex Murphy, who tormented and toyed with the best at Test match level in both hemispheres. Local rugby union players of ability were not allowed to linger too long in the fifteen-a-side game without the temptation of a cash offer to switch codes and, alongside Jeff Hitchen, Tom Pimblett and myself, county union players Peter Harvey and Keith Northey also made the short journey to Knowsley Road, while Cliff Watson responded to an advert placed by the club in a national newspaper.

Throughout the Coan years experienced club and international players were brought in from other league clubs to play their part in the development of the squad, with Wigan's Bill Sayer and Salford's Albert Halsall being especially prominent. There was even a recall for 'the one

who got away' in Barrow's tough, nuggety scrum-half,
Tommy Bishop. A sum of £5,000 was needed to return the
crafty number seven to his home town club and give him the
opportunity to become one of Saints' and Great Britain's
most effective and pugnacious half-backs. Although he later
found fame as a powerful international loose forward and
outstanding coach with Wigan, Widnes and Leeds, Doug
Laughton - as a youngster - displayed his undoubted talents
until a cruel knee injury and a far too hasty decision by the St
Helens directors to offload him on the transfer list, cut short
his blossoming career there. Only one young Australian,
David Wood, who came of his own accord and played less
than a dozen or more games, was listed on the Saints playing
register from '64 to '66. Some difference to today.

The talent available was plentiful, all a coach had to do to
achieve success was to select a team from it. Surprisingly,
though, in the Sixties, no coach at St Helens selected the team.

As with previous incumbents Alan Prescott and Stan
McCormick, when Joe Coan sat before the Saints' twelve-man
board of directors after training on a Tuesday night he could
only list the injuries and recommend his selections for the
match on the following Saturday. Quite often he and his
predecessors would be questioned on the merits of some of
the players before the self-appointed selectors around the
boardroom table would give their vote on the actual thirteen
players to line up in red and white jerseys. On some occasions
the coach would win the arguments, but often his preferences
would be challenged and even changed, frequently by men
who had little idea of the circumstances governing the coach's
choices. As Stan McCormick once revealed to me, a director
attacked him over the non-selection of prolific points scoring
South African winger Len Killeen for the past two weeks. Stan
had to explain how he had informed the board three weeks
before that Len, for personal reasons, would have to return

home for a month. The director, totally unaware that Len hadn't raced up and down the touchlines for the past fortnight, insisted: 'Well nobody told me where he was.'

No coach today - and rightly so - would tolerate such challenges to his rugby knowledge and authority, and nor would he consent to returning to the dressing room after his discussions to confront any upset player to try to tell him why he was not selected without revealing that he might originally have selected him. A farcical situation but one which often happened at Knowsley Road before the team sheet was pinned on the tiny notice board which adorned the wall of the first-team dressing room.

Whatever the selection dilemmas, the spirit within the club was a most harmonious one with few arguments occurring between players, coach or directors. And that atmosphere was no doubt partly responsible for the initial success when Joe assumed control. An unbeaten run of matches for the first four months of the 1964/65 season, a Lancashire Cup Final victory over our seemingly annual opponents Swinton and the winning of the Lancashire League and the new League Leaders Trophy was a fitting and deserved reward for the efforts put in by Joe and the team. But it was two defeats for which I remember the season, two losses which brought home to me how the reputation of any team and that of its players can often stand or fall on eighty minutes of play. Two setbacks which, despite the heartache at the time, taught me much and motivated me - and many of my team-mates - so that, twelve months later, we were in a position to enter our deeds into Saints folklore.

The Rugby League Challenge Cup and a visit to Wembley Stadium is still the highlight of most players' careers and is one occasion when they and the sport itself reaches out not only to a nationwide audience but to a worldwide one. It is an event which is ever in the thoughts of any ambitious player, but the realisation of them can often be determined or dashed in a matter of a few seconds in a nine month long season. So it was for me with St Helens in our two Challenge Cup campaigns of 1965 and 1966 and especially so at Central Park, Wigan in '65 before a 39,938 crowd, in the second round of rugby league's most prestigious trophy.

Any derby match between St Helens and Wigan, two rugby league mad towns separated by Billinge Hill and five or six miles of road, is an eagerly awaited occasion and invariably attracts one of the biggest crowds of the season. A meeting in the Challenge Cup adds even greater excitement and spice and so it was with this particular showdown which, in Tom van Vollenhoven, Alex Murphy, Len Killeen, Billy Boston, Eric Ashton and Trevor Lake, included some of the most exciting runners and try scorers in the game. For those who liked to see a punch up or two, there were a dozen of the toughest forwards around. Such was the anticipation for the match in both towns and the talent in both teams that Leslie Woodhead, the rugby league correspondent of the *Liverpool Echo* declared the game to be: 'A tie fit for Wembley, a game which would make the perfect Rugby League Challenge Cup Final. More international players will be appearing in this match than in any other second round tie.....a classic struggle is anticipated...... Wigan and St Helens are so evenly matched that forecasting becomes a difficult task......I am tempted to plunge for a draw.'

That his forecast of a draw proved mistaken was all down to those few seconds which can dash a club's hopes for the season. But the eagerly awaited contest did attract such a huge crowd that our best travel plans to the match were put to the test when our chairman, Mr Cook advised the bus driver to take advantage of the recently opened M6 link to Preston, by first driving north of Wigan before coming in to Central Park via a route supposedly not used by the hordes of Saints fans. Having been stuck in traffic for forty minutes before appealing for help from an escort of police on motorcycles, we finally arrived at the ground late and with little time for nerves.

The *Echo's* correspondent was almost correct in his judgement, so closely matched were the two sides. There was no score until two minutes before half-time when Wigan's Laurie Gilfedder gave his team a two point lead until Saints' Kel Coslett levelled the scores with another penalty goal in the 50th minute. With a ferocious contest underway between the two packs, it was left to the home side's superb ball playing prop Brian McTigue to deliver one of his famous short passes out of the tackle to Roy Evans, which allowed the loose forward to power through the narrowest of gaps in our defence and race away for the match clinching try. The tie summed up all that is best about rugby league, when local rivalry is at fever pitch and, such is the quality and reputation of the players, a near capacity attendance is guaranteed.

The second defeat which still scars my mind from that campaign was our loss at the hands of Halifax in the end of season Championship Final at Station Road, Swinton. It was a reverse which helped to motivate the team to achieve its 'annus mirabilis' a year later and a defeat which still helps to confirm my views on the ever popular debate as to what number of clubs should take part in a series of play-offs to determine the ultimate league champions, or whether the club which finishes at the top of the pile should be judged to be the rightful champions.

A 15-7 scoreline in Halifax's favour was hardly indicative of the two clubs' efforts throughout the normal season in which St Helens finished at the top of the then thirty club league table with just six losses and Halifax ended in seventh position after suffering eleven reverses. Many decried a system that allowed the seventh-placed side to become champions at the expense of the club which sat at the top of the league table. The same arguments exist today with some not in favour of a top eight play-off in the engage Super League to determine the Grand Finalists and the eventual champions. Even in defeat then, I was content to acknowledge Halifax's right to be declared champions via a sixteen team knockout tournament because, in a thirty strong league, sides did not necessarily play each other home and away or at all throughout the normal season. Hence it appeared only right that a club could challenge for the Championship in a mini-knockout format which excited the fans, aroused considerable media interest and attracted increased revenue.

The eight team format in operation today in the elite league encourages the same arguments but, again, I believe that the entertainment factor and the nationwide interest created by the staging of the Grand Final at Old Trafford, Manchester far outweigh the drawbacks. However, I would add a rider that the League Leaders trophy is upgraded and that, along with an extra substantial cash prize for the winning club, a major presentation ceremony is held at their ground on the day of its success.

Nevertheless, when the Halifax captain and centre John Burnett scored the first of his brace of tries in the opening half of our title clash, I realised that all was not going to plan and complacency, especially among the forwards, might prove our undoing. Though we hit back in the final forty minutes with a try and two goals from our winger Len Killeen, Halifax proved to be by far the better team on the day with the likes of forwards Ken Roberts, Terry Fogarty, Colin Dixon, Charlie Renilson and company subduing our own six man pack which had been expected to dominate and dictate play. It proved to be a sobering match in a season which had brought St Helens much success but it was a year which was to serve almost as an apprenticeship for me in what was needed if we were to win the ultimate in silverware. In 1966, it was two wins not losses, against one club - Hull Kingston Rovers - which were to provide the mental toughness, physical steel and the confidence to earn that Saints team a deserved place in the list of outstanding sides throughout its 115-year history.

Though I played international rugby against the premier nations of both codes and faced some of the finest club sides and players during my fourteen-year dual-code playing career, I can honestly say that the two matches against Hull KR, the first in the Challenge Cup and the second in the semi-final of the Championship, were the toughest yet most rewarding contests of my life. They provided me with the most committed and determined opposition I ever encountered in either code, while they created in me the greatest intensity of concentration and application and sheer bloody mindedness I have ever applied to any match. That commitment enabled us, eventually, to enjoy a most satisfying act of revenge on Halifax in the Championship Final. But firstly our battle with Rovers in the third round of the cup which included one of those occasions when again 'a few seconds' can determine or dash one's hopes for the season. The intervention of chance and a last throw of the dice from our midfield maestro Alex Murphy kept us on the road to Wembley.

The night of 4th April, 1966 was a momentous one that has remained in the minds of my generation to this day. For such was the drama in the closing seconds of the match, a precursor for the other titanic struggle a month later. Trailing by ten points to seven in the fourth minute of added time and physically shattered by the ferocity of Hull KR's defence, our exit from the Challenge Cup looked to be such a formality that thousands of despairing and disappointed St Helens fans had already left the terraces and grandstand and were making their way home on the red and white double decker buses which invariably lined up for custom outside the ground awaiting the full-time whistle. The Rovers coaching staff were screaming at referee Eric Clay to blow his whistle and when he did, wrongly in anticipation of the end of the match and a superb result, they leapt from the trainers' benches, raced onto the pitch and began to hug the players. But 'Sergeant Major' Clay was his own man and nobody would tell him when it was time to blow his whistle. Instead of signalling full-time and victory to Hull KR, he ordered a penalty to St Helens and, after ushering the irate and protesting Rovers staff from the pitch, he threw the ball to Alex Murphy.

There was no point taking two points from a penalty goal and arguments raged in the Saints ranks over what last-gasp option we might take in the hope of snatching victory. Mr Clay shrieked at us to make our minds up quickly as time had run out and whatever we did would be the last play of the match. Alex, unbeknown to all of us, at the same time as the referee's verbal blast, launched the highest 'up and under' imaginable onto the Rovers' line where Cyril Kellett, a lone sentinel at full-back, waited to catch it and clinch the game for his team. He dropped the ball and allowed it to roll towards the dead ball line or, as I - the next in line after Alex Murphy to get near the ball - have always believed, *over* the dead ball line. 'Murph dived on the ball and claimed a try before he, the ball and a couple of desperate tacklers went clattering down the players' tunnel immediately facing where the ball had been disputed. Pandemonium reigned. Eric Clay had never left the spot where he had awarded the penalty, some thirty-five yards away from the claimed try. Consultation with the touch judge was called for, even though he was probably further away from the incident than Mr Clay. Once discussion was completed, the ground was silenced while, dramatically, he walked slowly towards the Rovers' try-line to give his decision. All eyes were focussed on the right arm of the portly referee as he strode magisterially to the spot, everyone waiting to see whether he would point his hand to the floor and raise his arm aloft to signal a touchdown or wave at waist height in front of him to signal no try.

His hand pointed to the floor, the arm was raised in the air and the size of the roar of delight from the terraces caused many hundreds who had left the ground to leave their seats on the buses and to race back in to learn what had happened - we were still on the Wembley trail. The outcome brought forth accusations of cheating from the Rovers' players and their coaching staff and made for an uncomfortable half-hour in the communal bath after the match but, with the conversion kicked, it paved the way for our eventual Wembley triumph over our old derby foes, Wigan. It also meant a vengeful Rovers side returning later to face an equally determined bunch in one of the most hostile and brutal matches I have ever experienced.

There was more dissention ahead of the second match against the East Yorkshire outfit when the Rugby Football League decreed that the semi-final of the Championship play-offs had to be played on the Saturday night, prior to our appearance at Wembley. Hardly the ideal preparation for a Challenge Cup Final seven days later, and when I saw the expressions on the faces of our opponents as they climbed down from the team bus at the entrance to the Knowsley Road dressing rooms, and their reluctance even to say hello, I realised that this match would somehow be a little different to a normal weekly encounter. With over 20,000 packed into the ground and the atmosphere electric throughout, the door of the Rovers dressing room was shut with a loud bang and only opened when the players made their way to the pitch. They had served notice of their thoughts and their intentions. We were labelled as cheats. Before our own supporters we would be shown to be impostors in the Challenge Cup decider. But coach Colin Hutton and his men failed to realise just what steel was in the Saints team, especially when the gauntlet was so obviously thrown in our faces.

A 14-6 win, thanks to two tries and four goals from Len Killeen, earned us the right to go for the double but the manner of the victory amply illustrated the mettle of the side, its professional pride and refusal ever to back down. Journalist Brian Batty of the *Daily Mail* opened his account of the battle with the words: 'St Helens survived the fiercest test any team can ever have faced before Wembley to triumph in this bruising, injury-scarred semi-final.' He concluded his report by saying: 'St Helens move on to Wembley confident that no cup final can be a tougher task. As soccer's iron man, Jimmy Murphy of Manchester United summed it up, "there wasn't a coward among them."'

Another match reporter, Jack Paul, highlighted how, 'Leeds referee, Bob Appleyard, worked overtime pulling out player after player for lectures as fists flew frequently,' and revealed that 'St Helens last night were counting the cost of their semi-final top sixteen win against Hull KR...worried coach Joe Coan, listed his injuries: second-row forward John Warlow (badly concussed), loose forward Kel Coslett (hip damage) and stand-off Bob Prosser, who retired at half-time with loose teeth.'

Yes, it was rough. It was violent as Rovers' forwards led by Frank Foster laid into us with the thought that, faced with such ferocity just seven days from a possible appearance at Wembley, we would back off and save ourselves for another day. No such luck once, while John Warlow was receiving medical attention on the floor following the neatest of uppercuts, I had gathered the pack around me and asked if they were prepared to back down or stand up and be counted. They didn't retract a step but hit back hard - literally - matched by our fearless full-back Frank Barrow, who saved certain tries with crunching tackles on Rovers winger Mike Blackmore and centre Brian Wrigglesworth. It was Frank, too, who delivered the coup de grace when we were, ironically, again awarded a penalty in the last seconds of the match. My inclination was to let Len Killeen have another shot at goal so that no one would risk further injury before the final whistle was blown. It wasn't to be, for when Frank Barrow called for yet another 'up and under' in the direction of his opposite number Cyril Kellett, skipper Alex Murphy mischievously duly obliged.

On this occasion poor Cyril didn't even have the opportunity to catch or drop the ball for he was cruelly felled by Frank before it came down from the sky. Mayhem and fierce fighting erupted between both sets of players, the only exception being myself who whispered into the referee's ear: 'Bob, you'd be as well blowing your whistle for full-time. That'll make them stop fighting.' He did and that was the end of the bitterness between the players, all of whom relaxed, chatted and laughed together afterwards in the communal bath and happily bought each other drinks later in the club lounge.

Two defeats twelve months before had taught so many lessons. The manner and character of these two wins illustrated just how much we had taken on board from them; they were the springboard to a famous Cup and Championship triumph.

8

Up for the Cup!

WIGAN supporters and many neutral observers, when reflecting on their club's 21-2 defeat to St Helens in the 1966 Challenge Cup final, often heap the blame squarely onto the shoulders of Saints captain Alex Murphy for his supposed outrageous manipulation of the rules in the absence of the cherry and white's experienced hooker, Colin Clarke. St Helens fans insist that the victory was achieved by a fitter team playing a more skilful and powerful style of rugby against an ageing side no longer the force it once had been.

I have sympathy for both points of view but I would also add that the total confidence of the Saints players and the spirit and camaraderie built up over the previous twelve months - and especially during a week long training and relaxation in Southport prior to the Wembley showdown - contributed more to the win than the spectators on the terraces realised.

Whatever mine or the reader's point of view, the arguments of the Wigan supporters and the neutrals have held sway over the past forty four years. But Murphy's antics, all within the laws of the game, did not determine the result, they only contributed to it. Unfortunately for Wigan, Clarke was suspended out of the decider and they were forced to hand the number nine jersey to a young prop forward, Tom Woosey, who had very little knowledge of the rake's role. Ironically Saints, a month or two before the final, had signed their deadliest rivals' international hooker, Bill Sayer, for the derisory sum of only a £1,000 and Bill and Alex were intent on making Wigan pay for their blunder.

In the Sixties, any non-offending side were only awarded a kick to touch followed by a scrum after a penalty and, thus, it was far more beneficial for Saints whenever possession of the ball was lost. It clearly suited Alex Murphy's plans to hand Wigan a penalty by running offside whenever they were in possession and take the gamble of Bill Sayer outscoring Tom Woosey in the scrum count. That he did by sixteen scrums to eight, not as many as hysterical reports now insist, was enough of an advantage to allow Saints to monopolise possession and their position on the pitch. Alex Murphy was clever enough not to infringe the rules but he was astute enough to take advantage of them.

Such a glut of possession certainly helped St Helens to humiliate Wigan but the Saints team was a far younger, fitter and faster outfit than their rivals, who possessed some of the finest players ever to grace the game but were ageing and could no longer dominate as they once did. Skipper and centre, Eric Ashton, one of the greatest leaders of both Wigan and Great Britain and Billy Boston, the phenomenal Welsh winger and the scorer of an amazing 571 tries, were unable to spark their often match winning partnership and veteran prop Brian McTigue was never allowed to exhibit his magical ball handling control or display his powerful short defence breaking bursts down the middle. In contrast, we were told by coach Joe Coan to 'run the old men about the field' and his instructions were implicitly and successfully obeyed.

Saints were in control after only nine minutes when our ace Springbok wing Len Killeen kicked the second of his five goals from a staggering sixty yards out which put fear and foreboding in the hearts of the Wigan followers. Though the 'offside antics' did detract from the flow of the game, three tries from Saints illustrated the far superior running and handling abilities in their ranks. The first, begun by lively stand-off Peter Harvey and finished by international loose forward John Mantle saw Tom van Vollenhoven at his most elusive down the touchline. Not to be outdone, Killeen - the eventual Lance Todd Trophy winner for his man of the match performance - grabbed a touchdown in the 54th minute. A daring dive and twist in mid-air allowed him to catch and plant the ball in one movement, after a crafty grubber kick by his centre partner Billy Benyon. A further neat chip-kick and regather from the dynamic Tommy Bishop at scrum-half completed the try scoring, but not the agony for the tired Wigan players who had to suffer the final humiliation from their tormentor-in-chief Murphy, who claimed the final two points with a cheeky drop-goal from in front of the posts. A convincing win for a youthful and multi-talented St Helens team but one which, in my opinion, was fashioned more in the week before the Wembley showdown on the fairground, in the casino and in the palatial Grand Hotel in the holiday resort of Southport.

While Wigan's pre-Wembley training was carried out behind closed doors at their Central Park ground, the Saints players left for a week's training and coaching up the coast with instructions to train hard but also to enjoy the occasion. And enjoy it we did for though I doubt that any sports team of the era could have trained harder or worked longer during the hours spent with the ball on the thick green turf of the King George V School rugby pitches in Southport, at other times we were the most relaxed and carefree body of sportsmen. To be taken away to the seaside as part-time players for a week's training and bonding prior to the Challenge Cup Final helped to raise the profile and the significance of the whole event in our heads. And those minds not cluttered with the day to day trivia of daily life at home and work, concentrated all the more on what had to be done when the whistle blew for the kick-off on Saturday. No matter whether we were exhausted from racing up and down the sand dunes on Ainsdale Beach or shattered by the effects of practising move after move in a continuous eighty minutes imitation of the final, our activities away from the training pitch built up the amazing team spirit and camaraderie which is necessary to carry the best teams to their triumphs when all seems to be going against them.

A strict disciplinarian, Joe Coan also believed in the benefits of personal discipline and placed no curfews and petty restrictions on his players. His and my belief that an intelligent team must discipline itself if it is to capture success was put to the test and passed comfortably. Nobody kept a careful eye on anyone's movements and insisted what the players could eat or drink and it worked. What a week, what a preparation for our visit to Wembley Stadium.

Except that few of the Saints directors were ever aware how close they were to losing two or three of the club's renowned pack when the team decided to spend an hour on the boating lake on the Southport promenade. Only some frantic swimming and desperate paddling got prop Albert Halsall, Bob Dagnall and myself out of trouble when our happy go lucky full-back Frank Barrow decided to tip us out of our tiny paddle boat. And only the strongest of tree branches stopped Cliff Watson from crashing to the ground when, via window sill to window sill, in Spiderman fashion, he attempted to move four rooms down the corridor of the luxurious Grand Hotel.

Dinner at the Grand in the evening was the occasion for a formal, dignified gathering in a huge chandeliered ballroom attended by immaculately dressed, unsmiling waiters and accompanied by a trio of musicians whose repertoire was firmly placed in the 1920s and Thirties. Light relief did come for all when, at Albert Halsall's request, the trio concluded their version of 'The Blue Danube' and followed it with the popular hit of the day 'Hot Diggity' .To amuse the lads, I had arranged for Cliff Watson to place a screen in the centre of the ballroom floor, from behind which I appeared adorned in plastic flowers borrowed from the plant pots in the hotel foyer and two silk scarves kindly loaned by the receptionist. Oh yes, and wearing a jock strap.

To the music of 'Hot Diggity' and 'The Stripper', I entertained the players, directors and coaching staff to a sophisticated strip tease routine and received huge applause. Much louder applause than I expected and totally unexpected cries of, 'More, More!' issued from behind me where, to my surprise, a party of pensioners had rushed into the ballroom thinking that I was a part of the cabaret.

After that, it was out for our nightly visit to the Kingsway Casino Club and the temptation to risk a bob or two on the roulette and the blackjack, some with more success than others. Though Billy Benyon had a lucky run on the roulette wheel during the week and more than equalled his ninety pounds match winning pay on the Saturday, such was the losing streak of one or two of the team on the wheel that they were all the more determined and motivated to finish off the week with a win on the pitch.

I strongly believe that the bond between the players, the spirit and sense of humour fuelled by our trip to Southport and our companionship throughout the season were key factors in our success.

To achieve the double seven days later by also winning the Championship Final against our nemesis of the previous year, Halifax, was a different feat altogether and, surprisingly, one which gave me even far more personal satisfaction than the Wembley triumph. Played at Station Road, Swinton, there was no time for jaunts to the seaside to prepare ourselves. Nor was it right to attempt to do so for the Championship was then much more of a 'bread and butter' affair which needed a single-minded approach with light training at our Knowsley Road ground on just two nights of the lead up week. We also knew that we would be in for a tough encounter against a Halifax side which was travelling to the final on the back of ten successive wins and with a rough, rugged pack which, in Ken Roberts and Terry Fogarty, included two of the recently announced Great Britain Lions squad to tour Australia and New Zealand in the summer. The fact that Ken and Terry, admittedly two fine forwards, had been selected ahead of me - delaying my such selection for a further couple of years - filled me with anticipation for this encounter. As it did for my own pack-mates John Warlow and Albert Halsall, who also wanted to show the selectors why all three of us should not have been neglected. But we never expected the incidents and the furore which accompanied our 35-12 revenge win over the confident Yorkshire outfit.

Though our opponents led 7-6 on the half hour, we were so relaxed and feeling no stress at all after our victory at Wembley the previous week that few in the team were concerned. In the final forty minutes the fitness and extra pace which had swept all before it during the season soon proved too much for a frustrated and flagging Halifax side and Saints eased into an eight try rout including a hat-trick for Halsall and another trio of touchdowns and six goals for our prolific points scorer Len Killeen. What a sensation he proved to be during that incredible 1965/66 season with his points scoring feats including posting all the side's points in at least ten matches of the season.

Sadly the frustrations of the Halifax players and my, and some of my team-mates' determination to prove a point or two to the international selectors caused tempers to boil over. According to Eric Thompson in his match report for the *Evening Post and Chronicle* the mood was obvious from the kick off. 'Two tough packs sized each other up warily in the opening minutes like two heavyweight boxers sparring for an opening' until eventually, 'there followed a tough encounter in midfield in which Roberts felled Warlow in a manner of which Cassius Clay would have been proud.'

Battle commenced with even the fans to the fore in the shape of St Helens' own Minnie Cotton, who had stormed onto the same field a month previously brandishing her umbrella when her lodger John Warlow had been attacked in the Challenge Cup semi-final clash against Dewsbury. As Eric Thompson so graphically explained, tempers were a little frayed.

'Halifax second-rower Colin Dixon went looking for trouble... and in some subsequent skirmishes Murphy went warning him until Ray French came over and pulled back the Saints skipper with a restraining hand.'

But a real tempest followed to put a blot on the match with players from both teams, spectators, coaches and police joining in a 'battle royal' which was the ugliest I have ever seen on any rugby field. Minnie was in the thick of the fray once more, wielding her umbrella at a Halifax player and this time police officers were less ceremonious in the way they frogmarched her from the battle. 'It was a stand-up fight with punches flying all round in a pitched battle of players,' Thompson continued.

Ray French ...And Rugby

It was quite an event to bring the curtain down on one of the greatest seasons in the history of the St Helens club. No matter which clubs are involved in the two end of season finales, the atmosphere and the attitudes on and off the pitch at the Championship Final (Grand Final today) and the Challenge Cup Final are totally separate and do make for a different experience for both players and spectators.

The modern Super League Grand Final is invariably played out between the two best teams in the league and is usually a contest which displays all the intensity of approach and dedicated professionalism of the players and their coaches. Two sides, thanks to their performances over an eight month season, are battling to be crowned champions after a final eighty minutes, whereas those competing at Wembley Stadium for the Cup are there by way of winning four or possibly five knockout matches. The staging and the timing of the two spectaculars at Old Trafford, Manchester or the 'Theatre of Dreams' as it is known, and Wembley Stadium are significant in the contrasts surrounding both events. Played in the heartlands of rugby league and with an evening kick-off, the Super League showcase has become not only an attractive occasion but, because of the ease of travel for the fans, an extension of the normal league fixtures, albeit the most important match. The ground is essentially filled by regular rugby league fans and devotees of the sport who are looking for a good night out along with quality rugby. The Challenge Cup climax is a totally different event.

Wembley Stadium is an attraction in itself, as is London and, such are the surprises in knockout football, two clubs who have won little in recent years can emerge as the finalists and even the winners after a mere 400 minutes play during a season. Witness the success of Warrington Wolves and Huddersfield Giants in the final of the competition in

2009. The history, tradition, terrestrial media coverage, glamour and excitement surrounding the Cup elevates the tournament and rugby league not only onto the national stage but the international one as well. The encounter attracts a large proportion of neutral spectators from non-rugby league areas, while many supporters of the two competing teams take the opportunity to build a mini holiday around their trip to the capital. The atmosphere in and around Wembley Stadium is thus far more cosmopolitan than its counterpart at Old Trafford, while the rugby on the pitch often appears to be more relaxed with a greater emphasis on open play and free running in contrast to the forward orientated and tactical attrition often seen in a Grand Final. To play in one or both is the ambition of every player.

The current eight team knockout play-off format held in the weeks leading to the Grand Final does add excitement and drama to the end of a normal season and the presentation of the match itself under floodlights on a Saturday evening, complete with pre-match and half-time entertainment, captures the mood and interest of the fans. Accompanied by excellent media coverage, the event has far outstripped that of the Championship of my playing days and rightly deserves its place in the sporting calendar of major events. So, obviously, does the Challenge Cup Final, but I do feel that much needs to be done on and off the pitch with our code's most prestigious tournament if it is to continue to attract the massive interest it still does and maintain its current position of being a truly major, worldwide spectacle.

The Challenge Cup Final is still watched live in Britain by the largest crowd of the rugby league season and attracts more TV viewers worldwide than any other match. But I believe that a curtain-raiser played between the winners of a mini tournament of those Championship clubs knocked out in the earlier rounds would attract more fans to the stadium. In a rugby league world which today displays a massive gulf in ability, fitness and skill between the full-time Super League player and the part-time Championship ones, it is no longer possible for a major giant killing act to be performed by a lesser club at Wembley in the manner of Featherstone Rovers, Leigh or Castleford's deeds of yesteryear. The experiment with such an initiative in 1997, when Hull KR met Hunslet in a curtain-raiser, surely deserves to be repeated to allow any player the right to dream of performing at the famous stadium and to give the supporters of a weaker club the opportunity to cheer their heroes at a big event. More spectators would be attracted to the Final and the special family atmosphere at rugby league matches would be more evident.

Of considerable concern is the drop in crowds at the earlier rounds of the tournament, in particular because of the season ticket culture which now dominates the game. Many supporters, especially of Super League clubs, accustomed to gaining entrance via their cheaper season ticket, will not now pay out extra at top prices to watch their team annihilate a team from a much weaker division. Nor is the fans' interest and the momentum of the cup competition maintained when rounds are scheduled only once a month and often, between the quarter-finals and the semis, there is a two month gap; a situation which also leaves supporters barely three weeks to make arrangements for a day or weekend in London if their side progresses. Whether such fixture arrangements are the fault of TV scheduling or the Rugby Football League, some urgent attention does need to be given to the calendar. A staggering statistic highlights a seventy per cent drop in pre-final attendances between 1956 and 2006 with only a slight average increase over the past three years. A standard increase in the cost of season tickets across the three Leagues to provide vouchers for entrance to any matches at any venue in all rounds before the semi-finals would help to increase attendances and add to interest in the Final itself. The RFL did acknowledge the problem when they initiated free admission for Super League season ticket holders to their club's fourth round tie from 2009. An extension of the system for an added payment would not go amiss.

To ensure the future success of the Challenge Cup Final, the tournament itself might require some attention but the 1966 extravaganza at Wembley and the antics of Mr Murphy on the pitch certainly caused Mr Bill Fallowfield, the secretary of the RFL, to think seriously about the rules of the game. His deliberations and those of the members of the Rugby League Council over the next three months were, whether knowingly or not, to prove so dramatic that they changed the very style of play and the direction of the game itself. During the following season, they also created serious problems for me as captain of the all conquering St Helens team and especially its pack.

9

The Right Chemistry

AS we have seen, the Rugby Football League or, prior to that, Northern Union has never been afraid to experiment with the laws of the game. Invariably, because of rugby league's history of over 115 years of professionalism, most of the changes have been made to satisfy the demands of those who underwrite the game by their presence on the terraces, the spectators rather than the players.

A number of the most fundamental law changes which today still determine the difference between the two codes were all made before 1907, including the abolition of the line-out, the reduction to thirteen players per team and the introduction of the play the ball after a tackle. Such rules were introduced in an attempt to present the paying audience with a faster, more open and entertaining spectacle than rugby union, a game which, until the recent advent of professionalism, only needed to serve the interests of its players and could pay little regard to the wishes of those looking on. How times have changed.

Many within the corridors of power at the RFL's headquarters expressed their dismay at the manner of Saints' defeat of Wigan in the 1966 Challenge Cup Final. Few were more outspoken over our monopoly of possession and the manipulation of the laws and their weaknesses than the code's secretary, Bill Fallowfield. Within three weeks of Wembley referee Harry Hunt blowing the final blast on his whistle, Bill had ensured that the laws were amended and, within six months, had changed the face of the game dramatically by the introduction of the four tackle rule. On 9th June, 1966, the penalty law was changed to allow the non-offending side to take a tap after the kick to touch. Without a scrum, no longer could any budding Alex Murphy gain an advantage for his team by running offside with a view to seeing his own superior hooker regain possession of the ball from a scrum near the touchline. So, one of the most radical law changes in the history of the game was also introduced, firstly as an experiment during the BBC TV's Floodlit Trophy competition in October and later as a permanency in December.

The four tackle rule, first appeared on the Corporation's popular Tuesday night rugby league slot which saw my predecessor Eddie Waring commentating on a series of knockout matches. It was aimed at ridding the game of a team monopolising possession and, by virtue of the strength of its pack, winning the match without playing too much open and expansive running rugby. It was introduced essentially to increase the game's appeal to spectators and TV viewers and was increased to six tackles, six years later. When the lawmakers decreed in 1983 that the scrum after the sixth tackle be scrapped and the ball be handed over to the opposition, the modern fast and furious game of rugby league was born; to the benefit of the players as well as the spectators.

Sadly, however, for me, as captain of the St Helens side in 1966/67, the initial amendment proved difficult to come to terms with, especially with a law designed to put an end to the very tactics that had enabled us to win four trophies in the previous season. Little wonder then that my final full season at Knowsley Road proved to be a testing one and for many of my team-mates too.

Unlike the six tackle rule today, which is familiar to all players without any experience of previous versions of the play the ball and which is responsible for the constant and ordered flow of the ball between the sides, the four tackle version was a frantic and frenetic system leaving those under its jurisdiction with little time to develop unit skills or plan constructively any continuous attacking style of play. Four tackles, in my opinion, were simply not enough to allow a team to think tactically and the rugby on offer was merely a step up from touch and pass with many players often running sideways just to avoid the tackle or kicking the ball aimlessly and endlessly downfield in a frantic effort to move play from their try line. The new rule was certainly not satisfactory for a team like St Helens which had developed a heavy, powerful pack of forwards all of whom could run and handle well in midfield and, in the likes of Alex Murphy, Tommy Bishop, Tom van Vollenhoven and Len Killeen possessed some of the most gifted and prolific points scorers in the club's history. With an abundance of unlimited possession supplied from the scrums courtesy of either of two international hookers, Bob Dagnall and Bill Sayer, the Saints team was designed for the era of the unlimited tackle. Hence our coach and many players, including me, had to adjust to the new style of play which was quickly emerging but the laws of the game were not the only problems confronting Saints. Off the pitch, relations between our inspirational captain Alex Murphy, coach Joe

Coan and the board of directors had deteriorated over Alex's unwillingness to continue in the centre rather than in his natural position of scrum-half. His dalliance with a possible then record £12,000 transfer to an Australian club and, ultimately, his eventual exit from Knowsley Road as the Leigh coach in October '67 obviously resulted in the loss of a unique talent in midfield and a dynamism on and off the pitch. When he was not allowed to train at St Helens and, in return and despite my many pleas to him, refused to attend the taking of the team photograph recording Saints' history making winning of the four cups, I was appointed as the new skipper. Quite a task, especially so when Len Killeen, who scored an impressive 1,047 points between 1964 and 1967, began to harbour ideas of a move to Australia and eventually did sign for the Balmain club in Sydney.

The departure of Alex Murphy, since the day of my signing for St Helens one of my most treasured friends, was not only a huge loss to me personally but especially so to the club. His stay-away absence in the early months of the season undermined morale and, following the introduction of the four tackle rule fully in December of that year, cost Saints dearly for, if there was one player in the game who could have taken immediate advantage of the innovation it was Murphy; such was his speed off the mark, lightning reflexes and instinctive ability to launch himself through a gap in any defence. Yet, however onerous my appointment, I relished the captaincy and learned much which stood me in good stead when I moved on to Widnes. Nor did we readily relinquish our hold on the silverware available for, though Wigan and Salford were responsible for our shock exits from the Lancashire Cup and the Challenge Cup, we did manage to retain our hold on the Lancashire League Trophy and finished in fourth position in the league table, a position which allowed us to march on to a fierce

Championship Final battle with Wakefield Trinity at Headingley, Leeds and also, unfortunately, an embarrassing replay at Station Road, Swinton.

An absorbing contest on a rain sodden Headingley pitch resulted in a controversial seven-all draw which was only finally settled after a dramatic nerve-wracking goal kicking display from Trinity's international centre, Neil Fox.

Having to cope with some of the worst weather conditions to plague any Championship decider, referee George Philpott, was involved in two highly controversial moments when he disallowed what appeared to be a perfectly good try to our winger Tony Barrow and, in the 73rd minute, awarded Wakefield scrum-half Ray Owen a penalty try to level the scores. Nevertheless, whatever the rights and wrongs of Mr. Philpott's decisions - which sadly prompted such threatening and abusive letters for him and his family that he stood down in the replay in favour of experienced whistler Joe Manley - it was two goal kicks, the first an attempted conversion of Owen's late equalising try and the second a penalty shot in the final minute which are still vivid in my mind.

Neil Fox, the Yorkshiremen's giant centre, scored over 2,575 goals in an amazing twenty-three year career and yet, but for the intervention of the heavens, he would surely have topped that total if either of his two magnificent and brave efforts had gone over the crossbar and denied Saints a replay. Amid torrential rain and with hail lashing into his face he struck the ball as a peal of thunder and a shaft of lightning accompanied his attempt to convert Ray Owen's hotly disputed effort, from near the touchline. The ball lofted high and with great power, lightly grazed the far post on the outside and, dropping in the in-goal area, failed to trouble the scoreboard operator. As did his second attempt to win the match with another well struck penalty in the 79th minute.

Though Neil's uncanny composure and temperament in the foulest of conditions failed to clinch victory for Wakefield, they displayed their mastery of the newly constituted play to grab a well earned 21-9 win in the replay with a display of fast open rugby, particularly in the second half.

The season was over. It had been an emotional and, despite the team's comparative lack of success, an enjoyable one for me. Though I didn't realise it at the time, it was near the conclusion of my six years in a red and white Saints jersey playing with some of the world's finest rugby league players and, temporarily, the end of the club's insatiable appetite for trophies which had allowed me to collect a dozen winners medals courtesy of Lancashire Cup and League successes, Western Championship and League Leaders titles and Challenge Cup and Championship Final triumphs.

Never in my wildest dreams (or even nightmares) could I ever have believed that, within a couple of weeks of the opening of the next season and while happily painting the front of my house at the top of a ladder, I would be informed by the Saints chairman that he wanted me 'to go to Widnes.'

My handiwork around the bedroom windows was interrupted by my wife, Helen, telling me that Mr Cook was on the telephone and wanted me to see him at the ground. Not wanting to stop work on the painting of the window sills, I told Helen to tell him that I was busy and would give him a ring later. A couple of minutes later she returned and insisted: 'You had better speak with him. He says it is urgent as he wants you to go to Widnes.'

'Why does he want me to go to Widnes? Can't he go himself or get Basil (Basil Lowe, the secretary) to go for him?' I asked.

'I don't know why but he says you must be there before five.'

Intrigued as to why the chairman should want me to go

to Widnes, I climbed down the ladder, changed out of my paint spattered overalls and, thinking that he was about to ask me to do a favour for him by taking some message or equipment to the Widnes club, set off in the car for Knowsley Road. Not, though, before I had spoken to a passing neighbour about Saints' prospects of a win in the match against Swinton on the next day.

Some prospects, I didn't even play against Swinton for, within twenty-four hours of meeting with Mr Cook and eventually his counterpart at Widnes, Jim Davies, I was playing in a black and white hooped jersey for them at Naughton Park against Leigh.

Yes, Mr Cook certainly did want me 'to go' to Widnes, in an instant part-exchange deal for their stand-off and skipper Frank Myler. I was shocked and staggered by his announcement even though, in the harsh and often brutal world of professional sport, his argument that St Helens, full of talent in their pack, were desperate for some guile and leadership in the backs while Widnes were in a similar situation in reverse, was a sound one.

'What if I don't want to go?' I asked.

'Then the deal is off,' he replied. 'But it would be better for you and the club if you did join Widnes.'

The words 'better for you' somehow signalled to me that my situation could be difficult if I opted to stay with Saints and suddenly I felt like the meat on a supermarket shelf with a sell-by date sticker. I had captained the side through an awkward period and, confident that I was approaching probably some of the best years of my playing career for Saints, my pride was hurt and my further ambitions for the team shattered. Such was life in the Sixties in the part-time world of rugby league when a player, almost with or without his consent, could be sold off or exchanged for another in a matter of minutes.

Those career defining minutes spent in the secretary's office at Knowsley Road in the company of Harry Cook, Basil Lowe and the then secretary of Widnes Bill Johnson were, however, to lead to the most rewarding, satisfying and enjoyable four years of my rugby life. And yet, on that fateful Friday afternoon, after signing all the necessary transfer documents, I left the ground upset at the manner of my removal from the St Helens club and had little appetite for joining Widnes. Even more so when, on the next morning my great friend and colleague in the Saints pack Cliff Watson called at our house to pick me up in his car and take me to catch the team bus for the match at Swinton. Having not read the newspapers that morning announcing a 'Sensational Swap Deal', Cliff refused to believe that I would not be joining him in the car or the pack because I was preparing to pick up Dave Markey, Saints' young, pacy second-row forward who was also a part of the deal. If I had not almost pushed an incredulous Cliff out of my house, I would have been late for my first kick-off that afternoon with the Chemics, as Widnes Vikings were then known.

Invariably finishing in a mid-table position in a thirty club league during my four years with them between 1967 and '71, the playing strength of the Widnes club at that time would be considered today as being at Championship level. But the squad, with the likes of John Gaydon, Ged Lowe and Jimmy Boylan, had men who would have graced any Super League side. In Ray Dutton, Eric Hughes, Mal Aspey, Dennis O'Neill, John Foran, George Nicholls, Mal Aspey, Reg Bowden and others there was a crop of youngsters, many mere teenagers, who later were to become household names in the game and international stars of the Seventies and early-Eighties. My initial reservations surrounding my unexpected move were soon dismissed as I revelled in playing for a set-up which did, and still does, truly merit the accolade of being described as a family club. Such was the warmth of greeting, the care and concern for the players and the sheer passion and enthusiasm from the team for the success of the club that, when I later assumed the captaincy from half-back stalwart Ged Lowe, I felt honoured to be in charge. And, when you were the skipper of Widnes, unlike a captain today, you really were in charge of the team both on and off the pitch.

As a captain on the pitch at St Helens, I invariably had so many international stars alongside me that they often instinctively knew what was to be done or offered advice as to what decisions and tactics should or should not be taken or employed. In contrast, with so many talented and enthusiastic youngsters on the field at Widnes, I often had to curb their natural inclination to do too much themselves and had to direct play at all times and lead from the front. Off the pitch at Naughton Park, I regularly found myself in the role of social secretary for many of the teenagers and young players who appeared to be not too bothered about the professional aspects of the game and its win or loss wages but who simply wanted to appear in their home town's rugby jersey and enjoy themselves playing carefree rugby.

After any floodlit game at Naughton Park on a Friday night, within five minutes of the referee blowing the final blast on his whistle, only the likes of ageing warriors John Warlow, Jimmy Boylan and me were left sitting in the after match bath such was the rush of the youngsters to don their best suits and race off to the local night club in nearby Frodsham. I happily collected and banked a pound a week from all of them to pay for our end of season outing at Blackpool and sat alongside John and Jimmy on the bus as we made our way home at midnight without the teenyboppers and night clubbers. When the team bus was stuck in traffic and late for a fixture in Hull, and it was considered too late to stop for our pre-match meal, I had to order the driver to continue motoring around a roundabout outside Wakefield while I made half a dozen dashes between a café nearby for the pre-booked steak and chips. Having our secretary Tom Smith on hand to catch the food when thrown through the open door of the bus solved the problem of being unable to stop on the roundabout. It was me too who, when the committee had forgotten to book a meal before the match against Doncaster on a Boxing Day, had to apologise to everyone on the bus as I served lunch and handed out to each player two bags of crisps donated by the locally based manufacturers Golden Wonder.

As well as feeding the players, it was also the captain's task to limit their appetite if ever the feeding habit of one was affecting the diet of another. Such a task was allotted to me when an experienced and older member of the squad became accustomed to excusing himself from the last ten minutes of training on a Thursday evening in order to get to work on time for a night shift. Unfortunately, he developed a habit of also visiting the tea room above the bath and changing areas in the tiny Widnes clubhouse and there he regularly helped himself to at least half of the pile of roast beef sandwiches which were left waiting for all to enjoy after their exertions. Following heated complaints from the younger lads, I took it upon myself to visit the tea room before training started and, armed with a pair of scissors and half a loaf, I proceeded to cut a thin strip of roast beef from all of the sandwiches and carefully positioned the strips so that they were temptingly hanging out of the new sandwiches which I made. Nipping in, as usual, the culprit in question quickly grabbed half a dozen of the re-made sandwiches which, except around the edges were totally devoid of any filling, to eat during his break at work. He never excused himself again from training.

Whatever the nature of the job, a captain in my era at both St Helens and especially Widnes was in charge and it was to the credit of all the coaches under whom I played at both clubs that they expected their captain to play a considerable part verbally not only during the match itself but at training, before the game, at half-time and full-time. Rightly so, but a far cry from the situation today when an experienced coach like Wigan Warriors' Michael Maguire chooses to select his captain from any one of five senior 'team ambassadors' for differing matches or periods in the season. Or when a Super League coach opts for there to be two captains of the club at the same time!

I can understand any possible leadership problems created for a team if, under the modern interchange system, one of the twelve replacements from the four man bench happens to be the captain. But I do feel strongly that, given a contribution from one or two trusty experienced team-mates alongside him, there can only be a place for one captain in sole charge of a side. Despite being willing to listen to advice, there can only be one boss on the pitch and I firmly believe that individual responsibility within a club is helpful not only to making the captain a better player but is also, via respect for him from his colleagues, instrumental in instilling greater discipline within a club. As in the past, when the likes of captains John Whitely (Hull), Eric Ashton (Wigan), Alan Prescott (St Helens) or Derek Turner (Wakefield Trinity) have shown the way forward, in recent years Leeds Rhinos' skipper Kevin Sinfield, Warrington Wolves' Adrian Morley, Bradford Bulls' Robbie Paul and Huddersfield Giants' Brett Hodgson have dictated affairs and most often been the inspiration, tactician or quiet influence behind a victory.

Current supporters of Super League might well ask if clubs today have anything other than a captain by name only when they see water bottle carriers, trainers and even medics invading the pitch every few minutes at the request of a high profile coach to pass on messages to the players. Some of the intruders shadow a player giving instructions while play continues elsewhere on the pitch. How many times do a captain's eyes search for his coach seated high in the grandstand and a signal from him as to whether or not he should order a kick for goal when a penalty has been awarded? No coach would have passed instructions to Alex Murphy telling him what to do. If he had then I am sure Alex would have promptly told him what to do with the ball and where to put it. Thankfully for me the three coaches in charge during my time at Widnes - Joe Egan, Bob Harper and Don Gullick - though all so different, put their trust in a captain and were conscious of the values of the position.

Joe Egan, one of the all-time great hookers of the Wigan, Leigh and Great Britain packs of the Forties and Fifties, helped me considerably in making me into a more complete forward. His emphasis and advice on ball handling and close passing between the forwards and his calm, assured and softly spoken approach with the players suited me. He put great faith in his captains and gave them the responsibility and freedom they needed to become successful in the role. His successor Bob Harper, a former player and backroom assistant with the club over a number of years, trod a similar path without ever having the extensive knowledge which Joe had gained from playing all over the world at the highest levels. But Bob, such a genial and caring man, was prepared to learn from other coaches, different sports or even from other disciplines he had read about in books. It mattered not if a particular exercise proved a total failure and both mystified and amused the players.

How well I recall him taking me to one side before training to tell me of the latest book he had read concerning the study of isometrics and how a system of physical exercises embracing muscle tension could help the players with their fitness and mental well-being. The enthusiastic Bob insisted that such exercises in which, according to the

Ray French ...And Rugby

Oxford English Dictionary, 'the muscles are made to act against each other or a fixed object', would provide some diversion from our endless lapping around the pitch or sprinting on the track. They certainly provided variety, though of the music hall kind, I'm afraid. Standing on the pitch in front of a long line of Widnes players, Bob demonstrated how, if we placed our arms outstretched in front of us and constantly squeezed our fingers into the palms of our hands, while at the same time gritting our teeth and grimacing for three or four minutes, we would use up just as much energy as running a lap of the field. The novel routine would also, suggested Bob, freshen up our minds and provide a little light relief from the usual rigours of training. I looked at my veteran pack colleague John Warlow standing alongside me and asked him what he thought of such innovations. While keeping his teeth firmly locked together and maintaining a huge grimace on his face he declared: 'If we continue training like this, Ray, I think I've got another three years left in me.' Needless to say Bob abandoned his interest in that particular science.

Though few coaches were keener than Bob Harper, the former Saints centre of my boyhood, Wales international Don Gullick, was as widely read as him and probably on a far wider range of topics. During our travels to and from training together from our homes in St Helens by car, Don would regale me with the latest book he had been reading and insisted that I could learn much which would help me in my rugby by reading certain passages from them. Biographies of explorers, adventurers, scientists, philosophers, inventors, vagabonds, confidence tricksters, mountaineers and more were Don's staple diet and every week we met he would have a couple of pages of a book marked out and two or three paragraphs highlighted from the hero or villain's deeds, or thoughts from which I could learn. He loved his rugby and enthused me with his passion and devotion to it. He was well ahead of his time too in his techniques with his work with the many youngsters then in training at Naughton Park. In the Sixties and the early-Seventies, Don was one of the few coaches then concentrating on the individual skills of the players by working with them in small groups while most coaches of the era often assumed that because a player was a professional he should have already developed all the skills naturally.

The often eccentric but fervent methods of the coaching staff at Widnes helped me enormously to relax and widen my approaches to my own playing style and techniques. Surprisingly, too, the differences in outlook and relationship with the directors of both clubs also proved to be a strong influence in the development of my career.

At St Helens, although it was a relaxed one, as shareholders of the club the board had more than a passing interest in the team's fortunes and always needed to further the interests of the club often at the expense of the players – as with my own transfer to Widnes. Where a director can take a detached view and concentrate primarily on the needs of the club, is to be commended and it was the sheer professionalism of those at Saints and its winning mentality at the top which spurred on my progression during my six-year stay.

At Widnes the lesser pressures on a committeeman, voted on to the board annually rather than by invitation and the purchase of shares, were obvious. A far more relaxed attitude was the order of the day and, rightly or wrongly, more intimate friendships were developed between players, supporters club members and committeemen. All appeared to be working together for a common cause. On the way home from a good win on the team bus, we would often be led in singing by former Widnes hooker and committeeman

Jack Hayes, while local bookmaker 'Batty' Foran would often visit the dressing room at half-time to add a few more pounds to our pay packets if we were playing well and a win looked to be in sight. On the St Helens bus on the way home from a good win, the directors still read their newspapers at the front, discussed their next signing or considered whether or not the latest rugby union sensation in Wales could advance the prospects of the team.

The Saints chairman or the 'director of the day' visited our dressing room a few minutes before kick-off to every match and formally told us the size of the win bonus before rapidly making his exit.

The Widnes club in the Seventies and the Eighties, under the management of Vince Karalius and Doug Laughton and after the restructuring of their corporate governance, eventually became one of the most professional, successful and exciting in the history of the game. Their team was filled with stars of the calibre of Martin Offiah, Jim Mills, Jonathan Davies, Emosi Koloto, the Hulme brothers Paul and David, the O'Neill lads, Mike and Steve, Alan Tait, Joe Lydon, Andy Gregory and more. But it was the more amateur approach and the friendlier, relaxed attitude from coaching and management during my four years at Naughton Park which, while not rewarding the club with cups and trophies, gave me the responsibility, self-confidence and opportunity to achieve the international honours I had gained in rugby union. The casual chemistry both on and off the pitch was, strangely, more appropriate for my continued development and enjoyment and led to the fulfilment of my ambitions and for those many teenagers who also took their first steps to international recognition alongside me in a Widnes jersey.

10

Olympic Dream

FOUR years of rugby playing bliss. Little did I realise that, when I travelled home after making my debut in a defeat for Widnes against Leigh and feeling a deep sense of hurt and rejection over my transfer from St Helens, I would fulfil all my remaining hopes and ambitions in rugby league. Little did I appreciate too that, although I enjoyed a wonderfully happy career at Saints, performing alongside some lifelong friends who were among the world's greatest players in both codes of rugby, at Widnes I was to enter into the most satisfying period of my playing career. The very nature and background to my shock transfer between the two clubs provided me with an extra edge to my attitude and removed any complacency which constant success with Saints might have allowed to creep, unknowingly, into my game - most especially when playing against my old side and other major clubs. A third and the most personally satisfying aspect of my move to Widnes was the fact that, as a result of such changes, my form and playing style with the club eventually led to the captaincy of the Lancashire County side and my elevation to international honours and inclusion in the Great Britain World Cup tour party to Australia and New Zealand in the summer of 1968.

By virtue of playing, during the first five years of my rugby league career, alongside three of the fastest running second rows in the game in Dick Huddart, Jimmy Measures and John Mantle, my role naturally gravitated to that of the grafter, the tackler and the enforcer in the pack. Until, during the season of my captaincy in 1967/68, I played far more regularly alongside former Wales rugby union forward John Warlow, whose style of play was somewhat similar to mine. With the encouragement of Saints coach Joe Coan and taking on the responsibilities and leadership of captaincy, I began to play on attack more from the first receiver role and played a considerable part in the team's ball distribution in midfield. Though I always relished the constant graft required of a forward in rugby league and took great satisfaction from tackling and battling with the hard men of the opposition, I must acknowledge that it was the free licence given to my style of play at Widnes which resulted in my gaining international honours. And it was recognition from the media of my somewhat different performances in a Widnes jersey, particularly against St Helens, Wigan and the like, which gave me the most satisfaction and allowed me to prove to myself and many at the St Helens club that my enforced switch to Widnes had been a huge mistake.

In the early months of my career with Widnes, my heart ruled my head but as time moved on I soon realised the exchange deal involving myself and Frank Myler was a sound professional decision made by the Saints chairman and the best move possible for the two clubs and ourselves. The respective clubs prospered and both Frank's and my fortunes on the field blossomed from a change of direction and surroundings. But the realisation didn't stop me from focussing on any game involving Saints or a top team with the intensity of a cup final.

Local reporter Eric Thompson summed up my different approach when, following my captaining of Lancashire to a 23-17 win over Yorkshire, he wrote: 'Every Lancashire forward gave a more spirited display than I have seen from them for years but the one who surprised me most was the "new look" Ray French. This St Helens cast-off took over the Lancashire captaincy in sterling style, was slipping passes out in a character he never showed at Knowsley Road and is still his hard working, hard running self.'

Tom Ashcroft, the regular scribe for the *St Helens Reporter*, too, was surprised by my play when only a last gasp try in the final minute of a match in March 1968, from winger Les Jones, snatched a win for the Saints. As he kindly wrote in his weekly column: 'They were most ably led by Ray French who now has free rein and is not confined to the power game as he was in his Saints days. Thus we had him as the tactical kicker to touch, the undisputed pack leader and an example to all by his ability to get the pass away as he was being submerged in the tackle - an art which once mastered puts any forward into the top bracket. The French Saints fans once knew was obviously in a strait jacket.'

The transfer saga and playing for a then unfashionable club inspired me to helping Widnes beat St Helens on some notable occasions but my rekindled enthusiasm for the game and my desire to raise the ambitions of the youngsters around me, occasionally roused my passion for a win a little too high. Most notably, when I was given a police escort from the pitch and a dressing down by the chief inspector in the changing rooms after a good win over the then mighty Wigan. Though somewhat embarrassed by the intervention of the police, there was no way I was going to allow some slack tackling in the closing minutes of our 15-9 victory on a mud heap of a Central Park pitch when, in front of some irate Wigan spectators sitting on the ringside seats which surrounded the perimeter of the pitch, I gave a vivid verbal 'bollocking' to our right wing partnership. The upset Wigan fans reported me to the constabulary and surged onto the pitch at the final whistle as I was being led away and down the players' tunnel by two uniformed policemen. A visit from the chief constable to the changing rooms quietened down the incident but it wasn't the last I saw of him. Imagine his and my surprise when, on the following Monday afternoon, I met him again in my capacity as my school's careers adviser at a Police Careers Conference at the Hutton Police Training Centre, near Preston. A chat over a cup of tea and a promise from me to send him a couple of good rugby playing lads to join his police cadets soon settled matters.

With my playing performances and captaincy for both Widnes and Lancashire being praised by the media, it was not long before my name was being mentioned as a candidate for selection for the Great Britain team to meet France in Paris at the Parc des Princes Stadium in February 1968. However, after my chastened experiences of possible international selection five years earlier, I didn't pay too much attention to the clamour for my inclusion in the side.

In 1963 I had joined my Saints team-mate Keith Northey as a travelling reserve with the Great Britain side which met Australia in the Second Ashes Test at Station Road, Swinton, and suffered a then record 50-12 defeat. Being a travelling reserve to a team in the era before the introduction of substitutes and replacements meant that the reserve could only play if there was an injury to one of the selected team before kick-off but it was taken for granted that the reserve was very near to eventual selection. Not in my case though.

Scoring fifty points for the first time in an Ashes Test and registering a record twelve tries, Australia were in complete command against an injury ravaged Great Britain outfit and, although having every sympathy with my colleagues on the pitch, I did have high hopes that when selection for the Third Test took place within half an hour of the final whistle, my name would figure in the thirteen chosen. Especially since I had played no part in the debacle and had seemingly performed well my duties as a reserve in carrying the team kit bags and rubbing the players down with oils prior to the match. Surprisingly, thanks to the wise counsel of the thirty-man selection panel (the whole body of the RFL Council!) which met straight after the humiliation, I was not even included as reserve. What I had done to merit such exclusion I never found out. Perhaps I had carried the wrong kit bag or spilled too much oil on the floor and not on the players' legs. Whatever, I was banished from the fifteen-man squad without any explanation.

The announcement of the Great Britain side to meet France on this occasion brought me better news and I was delighted to be handed the roles of pack leader and vice captain under the captaincy of my good friend and former England rugby union team mate Bev Risman. It is amazing how our careers in both rugby union and rugby league have been so intertwined, playing together for the English Universities, Lancashire, North West Counties and England at rugby union, representing Great Britain together at rugby league and, in later years, liaising and linking together in many community, promotional and expansion ventures for the thirteen-a-side code at both amateur and professional levels. With Bev, a prolific points scoring full-back with Leeds, in charge on the field and Colin Hutton, an experienced and very approachable coach, in command off it I looked forward to the trip across the Channel with high expectations and a totally relaxed outlook in achieving my ambition of becoming a dual-code international.

Unlike my previous trip to Paris to take part in Bill Fallowfield's ill-fated experimental game against France, the clash in February '68 proved to be a most professional and disciplined job on and off the pitch. There were certainly no incidents similar to that of seven years earlier when our experimental team's forward, former South African RU player Ted Brophy, cleared a nightclub of all its guests by leaping on the stage, depriving a female striptease artist of a live snake which was firmly wrapped around her body and throwing it onto the floor among the shocked audience. A fire alarm ringing at full volume would not have cleared a room as quickly. Both Bev and I, watched by his famous father and legendary Great Britain RL Lions leader Gus, took advantage of a more disciplined atmosphere to our debuts and, following Great Britain's 22-13 win, were kindly praised by the *Daily Mail's* experienced league journalist Brian Batty.

'Bev Risman added another chapter to the story of his family's footballing success when he turned his Great Britain debut into a personal triumph by scoring 16 points at the Parc de Princes. It was fitting that one of the other British heroes was Ray French, the Widnes second-row forward, who played in the same England rugby union team as Bev before they turned professional. French, who was sold by St Helens earlier this season, was Britain's outstanding forward with his untiring tackling and improved handling. Both have now staked early claims for a trip to Australia with the World Cup party this summer.'

A hard earned 19-8 return win over France a month later on the muddy wastes of Odsal, Bradford, did indeed see Bev and I embarking on yet another rugby venture together - one which could and should have been accompanied with huge success but, thanks to mistakes made by the management, failed to realise our expectations.

Though the Rugby Football League and our tour manager Bill Fallowfield provided what was the ideal preparation on the pitch for coach Colin Hutton and his players, the arrangements for our departure to Australia proved disastrous. For the first time prior to any World Cup event, two trial matches were set up against Leeds and Salford which eventually resulted in convincing wins for the potential Great Britain tourists. A further practice match was held at Thrum Hall against Halifax with a Great Britain side including the novelty of St Helens' Springbok wing flyer Tom van Vollenhoven, a generous gesture and a tribute to his ten years of wonderful service to the code. All three matches helped to generate a good team spirit among the squad and created a better understanding between the players together in battle. So far so good but then came two crucial mistakes made by the management, which only became apparent when our aeroplane had touched down in Sydney and was made more obvious in the final twenty minutes of our opening clash in the competition with the Kangaroos on the city's famous cricket ground. I stress the words when our aeroplane had touched down for, during our agonising thirty-four hour flight, we appeared to be more on the ground than in the air. After leaving Manchester Airport on Saturday 18th May, we stopped at Zurich, Rome, Karachi, Calcutta, Kuala Lumpur, Singapore and Perth before arriving at our destination and eventually the Olympic Hotel in Sydney at teatime on the Monday. Such an arduous journey meant that we were set to meet a strong Australian team just four full days later. Did anyone at RL headquarters realise the time and preparation needed for a team before entering into what might possibly be the hardest and most demanding match of their careers? No, they didn't. We were certainly made to pay for that in the time prior to kick-off and eventually in the most vital match of the whole tournament.

My first training session in Australia on the Tuesday morning after our flight into Sydney is still vividly impressed on my mind and those musings don't give me much comfort. Having had virtually no sleep in a strange rickety bed in an antique lodging house which passed for a hotel close by to the cricket ground, within five minutes of starting our first training session on the field close by, I felt strangely tired and sick. I always considered myself to be one of the fittest of the players in any team in which I played but when, at the warm-up stage, I had slogged a few times up and down a hill on the edge of the training area I felt decidedly groggy and, along with others, was sick at the top of it. Throughout the training sessions over the next couple of days I felt lethargic and lacking in enthusiasm and was really concerned over my personal fitness until my pack-mates, Cliff Watson and John Warlow, informed me that they felt somewhat similar. None of us had heard of jet lag and few, I'm sure, understood the time needed for acclimatisation and training after a lengthy flight to the other side of the world before being ready to play in a major match so soon after. The organisers of the British section of the World Cup Tour certainly didn't and nor did they take into account the preparation needed on the ground Down Under before any visiting team can be truly ready for an equal contest. Indeed, the Great Britain World Cup party undertook a trip which was played back to front and only prepared the playing squad for the new domestic season when we returned home.

When any tour party visits the Southern Hemisphere, many of the players will never have played on the type of hard, fast grounds that are the norm, nor will they have handled a ball different to the one used in their own country.

Interpretations of the laws made by referees are often hard to grasp - a vital ingredient in determining the eventual result of Great Britain's opening match with the Green and Gold's in the '68 World Cup. Above all, before embarking on any Test Matches in Australia, a touring team needs to familiarise itself with the conditions of play by having at least two or three warm-up games prior to the big event. Instead of observing such a time honoured requirement, we journeyed around Australia after the main event to places like Brisbane, Mount Isa and Townsville, gaining wins over Queensland, North and Central Queensland while concentrating more on a daily diet of sun, sea, surf, sand and the occasional ice cold beer. We featured in a three-week itinerary of matches which should have been played as a lead into the World Cup itself, not just an enjoyable extra at the end of the seven-week trip and to give the farmers, miners and cowboys in the outback a chance to watch Great Britain on their doorstep. Such matches should have been used to mould a team before stepping up to meet Australia, New Zealand and France.

No matter, my first trip to Australia proved to be a most enjoyable one which not only further enhanced my playing career but nurtured in me the realisation that international competition was, and still is, the way forward if rugby league is to attain its deserving nationwide and worldwide recognition and enable it to stand in equal importance alongside other more media hyped sports. Whatever the problems on and off the pitch, I was ready for the World Cup and eager to sample the attractions and unique atmosphere of the Sydney Cricket Ground and especially the homely comforts of the Olympic Hotel, conveniently sited on a hill nearby and overlooking the famous cricket and rugby stadium.

Being an avid follower of cricket all my life and, as a

youngster, a keen listener to the Ashes Test series cricket commentaries which were devoured daily by my father and myself via a tiny, often crackling Rediffusion radio, I was naturally excited and honoured to be playing at the Sydney Cricket Ground. In fact, I would rank my whole experience of training and playing on the famous pitch as being the most memorable of my rugby career, even exceeding a visit to our own Wembley Stadium. I was in awe of the history and traditions of the cricket ground especially when, for the first time, I visited the small wooden changing rooms and made my way through the iconic wooden gate at the foot of the stairs in the Members Stand and onto the pitch. Though about to take part in a serious training session with the Great Britain squad and set to pose for the famous photograph which all Great Britain touring teams have had taken on the cricket outfield in front of the main grandstand, I could not get out of my head the significance of walking through that little, wooden brown gate and stepping onto the turf on which so many greats of the past had shone.

Images of legendary British Lions Harold Wagstaff, Jonty Parkin, Jim Sullivan, Gus Risman and others flashed through my mind as I opened the gate and held it in my hand for some time while I reflected on those league heroes who had, perhaps, paused for thought on the exact spot before moving on to perform great deeds. I was humbled to think that I was about to walk onto the pitch through the same gate as the likes of Don Bradman, Douglas Jardine, Len Hutton, Harold Larwood, Keith Miller and former St George rugby league player and Australian fast bowler Ray Lindwall. I could hardly take in the significance of my presence on the Sydney Cricket ground I was so overwhelmed by such notions and illustrious names of the past. I was even more impressed when I viewed the stadium on the morning of our opening match in the World Cup from the balcony of my room at the nearby Olympic Hotel. The very name, Olympic Hotel, has a distinction and aura about it that would indicate the kind of super deluxe five star hotels which seems to cater for today's rugby touring teams and which contain every amenity and hundreds of rooms. As a frequent visitor to such establishments with over a dozen touring sides covering games in Australia, New Zealand and elsewhere in the Southern Hemisphere, I have often found such hotels to be soulless and impersonal and hardly ideal for creating a team spirit and a sense of unity among any large squad of players. Not so the Olympic Hotel, which was in fact a typical Aussie bar/lodging house situated on the corner of a street. With three players to a room, a sink and one large seemingly second hand wardrobe between them and a lounge area downstairs which was shared with the Aussie workers who filled the bars on their way home from work at five, the Olympic was far from being a salubrious residence. Its culinary delights - a choice of spam and eggs or corned beef and eggs offered for breakfast every morning - were somewhat limited when compared to the diets of the modern rugby player, but the venue was ideal for any touring team which wanted to bond and develop a spirit and a camaraderie which has lasted to today.

No player looking over at the Sydney Cricket Ground at ten on the morning of the opening match, as John Warlow, Cliff Watson and myself did from the balcony of our hotel room, could fail to be aroused by the sight of an almost full stadium and ever increasing queues of fans circling outside. We could not avoid the intensity of the atmosphere and the banter in the saloon bars, hallways and lounges downstairs as the Aussie supporters began their drinking for the day while we tucked in to our spam or corned beef delicacy. Few players lacked the concentration needed for a game when, on leaving the hotel at around midday, they walked down the back street to the ground mingling with crowds of Aussie supporters, many carrying their cooler boxes stacked with ice cold beer and letting us all know their views on the possible outcome of the game. Such simple pre-match preparation and our lack of transport to and from the ground might be looked upon with shock and even horror today by the ever increasing array of players, coaches, conditioners, managers, video analysts, statisticians, physiotherapists, dieticians and the like who accompany a modern touring party. But, regardless of the eventual outcome of our World Cup odyssey, I do believe that the now seemingly apparent limitations and inadequacies of the Olympic Hotel provided our Great Britain squad with benefits which are missing from the preparation of international players in 2010. Sadly, however, our treasured experiences still did not enable us to beat Australia but the matches, atmosphere and interest surrounding them instilled in me my strong belief that meaningful international expansion and competition is the only way forward.

11

International Rescue

THE noise of a capacity 62,256 crowd packed into the Sydney Cricket Ground hardly troubled our Great Britain team as we sat on the wooden benches in the away dressing room listening intently to the words of Mr John Percival the Kiwi referee who was to be the man in the middle for our opening clash in the World Cup with Australia. Even Tommy Bishop and Roger Millward had stopped chattering as, at the request of manager Bill Fallowfield, the man in black was talking us through and using myself and Bev Risman to illustrate just how he wanted us to play the ball during the game. Such a lecture and exhibition from the New Zealand whistler had been initiated by Bill to guard against any confusion over rule interpretations even though he naively insisted: 'We don't expect any major problems whatever. Any differences in interpretations will only be very minor and our boys should have no trouble adjusting to them.' Thanks for your famous last words, Bill!

Having instructed us in a most authoritative tone and in

strict schoolmasterly style, Mr Percival left the dressing room and, having penalised our hooker Kevin Ashcroft at the first play the ball, continued to do likewise to Great Britain for the same offence with such regularity over the next eighty minutes that the Australian full-back Eric Simms was able to grab a then world record eight goals in an Anglo/Australian Test, and guide his side to a 25-10 win. Such was the influence of Mr Percival's whistle on the game and his insistence on marching Great Britain back another ten yards whenever anyone dared to question his judgements, that the former Aussie centre legend Reg Gasnier was moved to say after the match: 'Thank goodness he isn't an Aussie.'

Though our rhythm was upset by the constant interruptions in play and many of our players, including me, in the final quarter did feel the effects of our long transit to Sydney, we were beaten by a more determined team. Two excellent tries from Ian Brooke and Clive Sullivan couldn't hide the fact that we had indulged in too much lateral running and employed too many well rehearsed moves rather than taking the Aussie pack on upfront in the early stages to gain dominance in midfield. With our fiery scrum-half Tommy Bishop playing strongly and distributing the ball well, the enthusiasm of our forwards kept us on equal terms until late on when the drives of Artie Beeston, Ron Coote, Dick Thornett and the outstanding John Raper broke our resistance. A cheeky dummy and a powerful thirty yard burst down the middle of the pitch, which resulted in a try between the posts for Raper, finally sealed our fate.

Naturally upset by our defeat, my spirits were boosted by the fact that many in both the Aussie and English media reported that I had played well with former Kangaroos' hard man prop Noel Kelly insisting in his newspaper column: 'Karalius would have wept! I never thought I'd be wasting my sympathy on any Pommy forward but I couldn't help feeling sorry for their one-man pack, Ray French, last Saturday. The way he was crucified by his team-mates up front would have made blokes like Vince Karalius, Rocky Turner and big Jack Wilkinson weep blood.'

So much for the praise for within forty-eight hours I was shocked to learn from Bill Fallowfield that I had been left out of the next match in Auckland against France because, as he said: 'You did too much on your own. We are aiming for a different style of play on Saturday.'

Our style of play against Australia had been, to my mind, too much akin to touch rugby and with little enough of the aggression needed against the Aussies, who will walk all over you if you allow them. Despite being hurt at my non-selection for our second match of the tournament, I joined in wholeheartedly at training in wet and windy Auckland and did my best to help maintain the good spirit which was still evident in the squad. Sadly for Bill Fallowfield and Colin Hutton, the team they selected never had any chance of playing a different style of rugby against the French when they were confronted with gale force winds, driving rain throughout and a Carlaw Park pitch covered in such thick, cloying mud that youngsters carrying buckets of water had to step onto the pitch at regular intervals to allow the players to wash it away from around their eyes.

Over 18,000 brave souls suffered the inhospitable conditions the majority of who, like me, must have realised that whichever side managed to score a try would emerge as the winner. France did just that and claimed a deserved 7-2 victory.

While I strived to keep warm and dry while sitting on the wooden bench alongside the touchline reserved for our coaching staff, my team-mates struggled to cope with the atrocious weather and failed to adapt to the foul conditions underfoot. Attempting to play too much rugby in conditions which warranted a far simpler approach, Great Britain floundered and could only trouble the scoreboard operator with a lone Bev Risman penalty goal. Throughout the eighty minutes play the French, led up front by their veteran front-rower and captain Georges Ailleres, settled for the simple but effective tactic of merely kicking the ball as high and as far as they could whenever they were in possession of it. Although not very entertaining to watch, their ploy paid dividends when winger Jean Ledru took advantage of a mistake near to the Great Britain try line and touched down for what was eventually to prove the only try of the match. A despairing GB had squandered possession by throwing and then constantly dropping the slippery ball along the backs when near to the French line.

The result was an embarrassment for us and we were rightly heavily criticised in the press for our far too ambitious tactics. France were set to play Australia in the final while we were facing the possible humiliation of losing all three matches in the World Cup when, a week later, we lined up against New Zealand before a sparse 14,000 crowd scattered around the grassy banks and almost deserted grandstands of a forlorn looking Sydney Cricket Ground. I especially and my team-mates had much to prove to our critics but little did I know that, after enjoying almost forty minutes of my best and most carefree rugby on the tour, I would be forced to make a dramatic exit from the action and take no further part in the match.

Enjoying the hard dry cricket ground underfoot and a crisp but sunny day in Sydney, our backs at last had the opportunity to show their ability with flying winger Clive Sullivan helping himself to a hat-trick of tries alongside others from Ian Brooke, Mick Shoebottom and Alan Burwell with a brace. Also enjoying the free running, all out attacking style, my second-row partner, Featherstone Rovers' Arnie Morgan, added another try while Bev calmly contributed seven goals to a comfortable 38-14 winning score line. Unfortunately I have little recollection of some of those tries.

I had much to prove to those who had omitted me from the side to play France the previous week and was certainly revelling in the fast open play in the first half. Thanks to some perfectly placed defence splitting passes by loose forward Charlie Renilson and ineffective tackling by the Kiwi forwards in midfield, I was able to make a good number of breaks and link into many handling movements. I really was relishing the action until, just seconds before the whistle for half-time, I was despatched from the field by one of the finest executed short arms I have ever seen - or, more accurately, been told about. Galloping for the line with only the New Zealand full-back Doug Ellwood in front of me and with Tommy Bishop alongside waiting for the final try scoring pass, I was suddenly felled from behind by a blow at the side of the chin from a covering New Zealander. My senses were no longer with me, my legs had no feeling in them and I hit the floor like the tiring heavyweight boxer who has been caught in the last round by his opponent's favourite uppercut punch. After almost exhausting a bottle of smelling salts, three minutes later I was helped off the pitch and back to the dressing room through the small wooden gate which had, three weeks earlier, so filled my mind with memories and heart with glee. On this occasion, I couldn't even recall our substitute Cliff Watson passing me on his way out to take my place in the team.

My World Cup was over, Australia became champions by virtue of a convincing twenty points to two win over France and I and my colleagues were left to enjoy our jaunt through Queensland. I use the word jaunt to describe the final two weeks of our tour because, being free from the pressures of Test match rugby, we were able to relax on and off the pitch and, against lesser opposition, could play some entertaining rugby. It was then, in places like Mount Isa, a small town lying in the outback and situated in one of Australia's biggest iron ore and uranium mining areas; in Brisbane, a beautifully laid out city straddling the banks of the local river and in the intensely competitive sporting arena of Sydney and its famous Cricket Ground that I fully realised the importance, significance and value of international competition for the fulfilment of a player, the satisfaction of the fans, the interest of the media and, above all, the very credibility and profile of the sport itself.

Thanks to the entrepreneurial zeal of Wellington businessman A.H. Baskerville, who inspired the New Zealanders' tour of Britain in 1907/08, and Sydney-born James Giltinan, who organised the first visit by Australia twelve months later, international rugby league was established. Even though Great Britain reciprocated the visits with a trip by the inaugural British Lions RL party in 1910 under their legendary captain Salford's James Lomas, the code's further development worldwide was effectively still-born for the next seventy years at least. The educational and social advantages held by rugby union, the blatant and often legally backed hostility to the spread of the thirteen-a-side version and at times the very parochial nature of the rugby league fraternity proved too much for a game which was vilified for its adherence to semi-professionalism and, as a result, considered by many to be socially inferior to the supposedly amateur ethos of its rival.

In their book, *Centenary History of the Rugby Football Union*, the authors U.A. Titley and Ross McWhirter outline the speed of the game's international development made both before and following the great split in 1895. They have

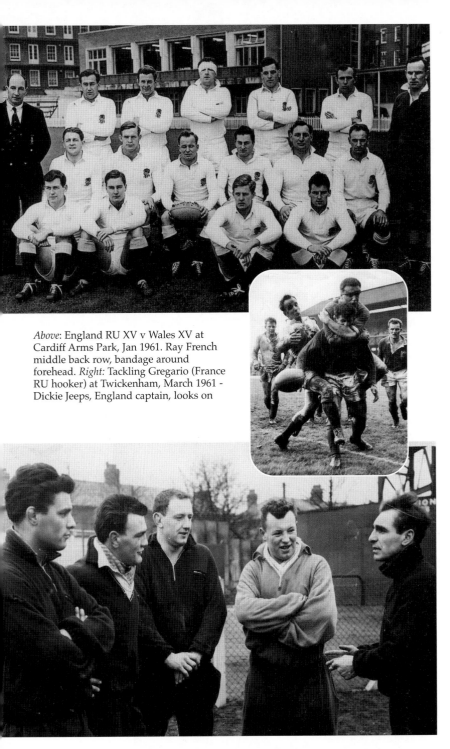

Above: England RU XV v Wales XV at Cardiff Arms Park, Jan 1961. Ray French middle back row, bandage around forehead. *Right:* Tackling Gregario (France RU hooker) at Twickenham, March 1961 - Dickie Jeeps, England captain, looks on

Above: St Helens coach Stan McCormick passes on advice to four young forwards. Left to right - Mick Knowles, Cliff Watson, Ray French & Keith Ashcroft in 1963

Above: Vince Karalius & St Helens celebrate with the Lancashire Cup 1962/63. Ray French is pictured back row, second from right

Left & below: In the thick of the tackling action with St Helens - the hometown club I doted on from being a boy

Left : In the thick of it against Huddersfield

Above: The all-conquering St Helens team of 1964/65, including rugby league greats Cliff Watson (fourth left front row), Tom Van Vollenhoven (seated first left front row), Alex Muprhy (centre front row), pictured with trophies won

Left : Scoring the winning try in the Western Championship Final at Central Park versus Swinton in May 1964 - Saints 10 Swinton 7...

Below : ...& against Liverpool City

Below: Jubilant St Helens players hold skipper Alex Murphy aloft after their 21-2 win over Wigan in 1966

Left: Ray French of St Helens tries to break through against Wakefield Trinity. May 1965

Above: St Helens winners of four trophies 1965/66. League Leaders Trophy, Lancs League Trophy, Challenge Cup, Championship Trophy, Lance Todd trophy (Len Killean). Skipper Alex Murphy is absent

Below: Getting my hands on the rugby league Challenge Cup

Above: All smiles with good friend Eric Ashton, Wigan skipper, whose outstretched arm had been mistaken for a short arm tackle by referee Mr Hart

Above: The first ever sponsorship of St Helens prior to the 1966 Cup Final. We were each given a free string vest by a local retailer and the opportunity to buy another for 7/6d!!! Left to right - back row: Kel Coslett, Bob Dagnall, Frank Barrow, Ray French, Tony Barrow, John Warlow, Billy Benyon. Front row: Tom van Vollenhoven, Albert Halsall, Peter Harvey, Bill Sayer, Alex Murphy, Tommy Bishop, Cliff Watson

Left: Referee monsieur Lacage of Bordeaux attempts to sort out the trouble after I am poleaxed by a high tackle during Great Britain's 19-8 win over France at Odsal, Bradford, March 1968

Below: The Great Britain team to face France at Parc des Princes, Paris, in February 1968. We won the Test match 22-13

Left: Sydney Cricket Ground, GB v Australia in the 1968 World Cup Charlie Renison (Halifax), Cliff Watson (St Helens) & Ray French (Widnes)

Below: Paying a return visit to the Olympic Hotel, home of Lions parties in Sydney for many years

Above: Pictured with the media corps on tour with the 1988 Lions down under. Left to right: Paul Harrison (The Sun), Jack McNamara (Manchester Evening News), Alan Thomas (Daily Express), Paul Wilson, Brian Batty (Daily Mail), Peter Wilson (Daily Star) and Ray French (Today & BBC) in Sydney

Left: Launch of my earlier book - *100 Great Rugby League Players*, supported by Duggie Greenall, Kevin Tamati, Stan McCormick, Alex Murphy, Alan Prescott & Eric Ashton

Right: Teaching the art of rugby union scrummaging at Cowley School, St Helens

Below: On tour with Cowley School in South Africa in 1991. Here the kids and coaches line up in Kagiso township, Johannesburg

Above: Scuba diving off the coast of Papua New Guinea, near Lae, in 1990 with my fellow dual-code internationals John Devereux & Jonathan Davies

Right: I've still got it! Playing for the media team in a Leeds Rhinos sevens tournament at Headingley while 65 years old

Above left: Interviewing Great Britain half-back Bobbie Goulding for the *Today* newspaper on tour in Fiji, October 1996. Bobbie bagged a record 32-point haul of three tries & ten goals

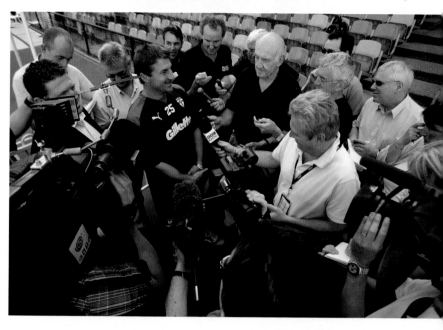

Above: Ray French in the middle of the media scrum grilling then England coach Tony Smith, during the 2008 Rugby League World Cup in Australia

no doubts as to the reasons for it and the problems confronting the then Northern Union. As they insist: 'Outside Great Britain, it was enthusiastic businessmen and the Armed Services who originally pioneered rugby football in so many parts of the world. In fact the Services did more than any other agent to "sell" the game everywhere, even in the most unlikely of places... a game between Military and Civilians on August 28th 1862 was probably the first organised football match played in South Africa...and the advance of France to world status owes much to crews of ships of the Royal Navy visiting ports down the west coast and into the south where France's principal rugby strength came to be concentrated.'

Some likelihood of rugby league prospering abroad when the playing of it, unlike all other sports, was banned in the Armed Forces. Fat chance of French Rugby League maintaining its dominance over the union game in the late-Thirties when the code was banned by the Nazis and union-minded quislings, in the Vichy Government in 1941. When later released from such draconian measures, French league was not able to use the word 'rugby' when referring to the game, instead being forced to use the title 'jeu a treize', signifying 'a game for thirteen'. What hope of any player trying their hand at the attractions of rugby league when, for over a hundred years, until the intervention in Parliament of a number of determined MPs of a rugby league persuasion, they would be banned from returning to the considered pure code of rugby?

An even bigger obstacle to the development of rugby league, however, was and still is the difficulties in overcoming the advantages handed to rugby union by the dominance of the sport on the playing fields of our public schools and the grammar schools.

The league code, especially in the immediate years after

the breakaway in 1895 and to a considerable extent until the advent of Super League and full-time professionalism, served the needs of miners, glassworkers, manual labourers, local government officers, teachers and others whose employment was invariably within their local town's borough. In stark contrast pupils on leaving the public schools, grammar schools and, ultimately, the universities had an education and training which allowed them to use their intellectual capabilities far and wide. No surprise then that, when many such graduates furthered their careers abroad in the public and private offices of countries like Singapore, Hong Kong, South Africa and their ilk, they promoted and supported the game they had been brought up with. While the league code became exceptionally strong and well supported within its own self-serving base, the union one flourished worldwide. Only in Papua New Guinea, where rugby league is the dominant, national sport, have we seen similar circumstances of development to that experienced in union. As already described, the staging of a series of friendly rugby league matches in PNG's capital city Port Moresby in 1949 between a team of civil servants working for the Australian government and another selected from the city's business and banking community, attracted the interest of the local inhabitants. And, thanks to the sporting interests of the Aussie civil servants, bankers and businessmen, rugby league was introduced to a native population keen to adopt it as their own game.

How times have changed at our universities and colleges where, until 1968, the sole game played with an oval ball was of the fifteen-a-side variety. Today, with rugby league available at all and with international student competitions being played worldwide, there is no shortage of league converts to spread the gospel whenever and wherever they take up employment. It is surely no coincidence that, since the introduction of rugby league into the Armed Services, the higher education establishments and even many sixth form centres nationwide has come on board. The provision of a free gangway between the two games is another factor why there has been growth and interest in league worldwide over the past fifteen years, much greater than has been the case over the previous century. Similarly now, at spectator and administrative levels, league is well on the way to attracting a similar social strata to that embraced by its rival.

Rugby league has, in the past, often been too inward looking and too obsessed with its parochialism and, especially in the Forties and the Fifties when crowds at matches were at an all time high, occasionally too smug and self-satisfied to bother to extend its boundaries. Indeed I am often reminded of William Shakespeare's words offered to Brutus in his play *Julius Caesar* whenever the topic of expansion in rugby league is discussed:-

'The fault, dear Brutus, is not in our stars,
But in ourselves, that we are underlings.'

But few can fault the enthusiasm and the success of the many development officers and volunteers who are now spearheading the surge of rugby league abroad. When one reads of a schools match played in 2010 between Qatar English Schools and a Lebanon under-16s Select and a first ever clash between a Saudi Schools Select and a Lebanon side in Tripoli, it is obvious that rugby league is at last on the move.

Though the move to summer rugby for our professional players means that the two premier leagues in Britain and Australia now run concurrently and provide for severe restrictions on the continuance of the well established and much followed RL Lions tours Down Under, the introduction of the annual Four Nations Tournament in the months of October and November featuring England, Australia, New Zealand and either France, Wales, Scotland or Ireland or one of Papua New Guinea, Fiji, Tonga, Samoa and the Cook Islands, depending on whether the competition is being staged in the Northern or the Southern hemisphere, is a welcome alternative. The pyramid of European Cups and Shields featuring the likes of Scotland, Wales, Ireland, Russia, Serbia and Lebanon is a satisfying second tier tournament providing international competition and development for those players in virgin territory still coming to terms with the demands of the game, by playing with and against a handful of leading Super League or NRL players. With club sides and national teams now featuring in over thirty countries including USA, Ukraine, Latvia, Estonia, Jamaica, Germany, Italy and elsewhere the outlook for international exposure for fledgling league playing nations is now far rosier than at any time in the code's 115-year history. The success of the 2008 World Cup held in Australia and the promise to come from a similar fourteen-nation tournament already scheduled to take place in Britain in 2013 and, most likely, Australia in 2017 is at last beginning to provide the income and the credibility to underpin expansion below the top tier of nations.

International expansion and competition between rugby league playing nations at all levels is the way forward to satisfy the players, spectators, media and the very game itself. While commentating for BBC TV on the 2008 World Cup, I will never forget the size of the smile on Stanley Gene's face and the exuberance displayed by his team-mates when Papua New Guinea took the lead against England in the clash at Townsville. Moreover, I will always recall the determination and passion of the Irish team when faced with the might of Samoa and Tonga. If any players exemplified what it means to play for their country or even adopted country, the Irish players did and the attitude and abilities of all benefited from their international exposure. I well remember too the happy smiling Fijian fans in the crowd at the Sydney Cricket Ground proudly wearing their traditional dress and roaring on their favourites against the might of Australia, and let me give the highest praise to the many thousands of English supporters who travelled out to Australia and maintained their good humour and unswerving support despite their team's poor performances on the pitch. Players of the calibre of St Helens' Francis Meli, Parramatta's Jarryd Hayne, Wigan's George Carmont, Willie Manu from Hull, Brisbane Broncos' Ashton Sims and others were able to represent their Pacific Island nations and feel proud to do so.

The deeds of such teams and their players and the mass media coverage of international events by terrestrial and satellite TV, Radio, the Internet and, of course, newspapers is vital to the promotion and profile of rugby league in all countries. Many league devotees quite rightly moan about the all too often sparse coverage of our game in many of the nationals and occasionally rage at the treatment afforded by certain news outlets in the south. But we must realise that, although the outcome of matches between Hull FC and Hull KR, Saints and Wigan Warriors or Leeds Rhinos and the Bradford Bulls will attract big crowds and interest, it is international competition and global tournaments which arouse the interest of a larger audience nationwide. International contests attract and tempt those who support their nation whatever the sport and can be a vital way in for exposing them to it. Leading players can only receive the income and celebrity status they desire and be reassured to stay within rugby league and not switch codes if they are regularly tested at the highest level on the representative stage. International events can hardly be ignored by the media, especially if England or a British team is successful. It is not twenty years ago since the likes of Martin Offiah, Ellery Hanley, Garry Schofield, Shaun Edwards, Andy Farrell, Jason Robinson, Joe Lydon, Jonathan Davies and company were performing in a red, white and blue Great Britain jersey before 50,000 and 70,000-plus crowds in a Test match or World Cup Final at Wembley or Old Trafford.

The Rugby Football League and the International Federation is right to concentrate on placing the emphasis in our game on international events at differing levels for, regardless of the small pockets of still parochially-minded fans at grassroots level, it is the only way to expand our game's horizons. It will also ensure we catch up with the development policy always so effectively pursued by the Rugby Football Union.

12

A Developing World

WITHIN four years of the 1968 Rugby League World Cup, the first of my fifteen visits to the Southern Hemisphere, and after playing in almost four hundred matches in a ten-year career in the thirteen-a-side code, I dramatically began to widen my own international horizons. Thanks to my increased commitment to schoolboy rugby at Cowley School in St Helens, my appointment as rugby league correspondent for the *Today* newspaper and, ultimately, my commentating roles for BBC TV and BBC Radio Merseyside, the past forty or so years have proved hectic. But, with every discipline, whether teaching English or Latin, coaching, writing on rugby or broadcasting worldwide over the airwaves, I have enjoyed every minute of the experiences and feel privileged to have been allowed to indulge myself in the passions of my life.

I am fortunate to have been given the licence to involve myself fully in every job, often at the same time, by a number of understanding and sympathetic headmasters, sports editors and radio and TV producers. I fondly recall an advert from yesteryear urging Britain's youth to 'Join the Navy and see the world!' Well, I have only crossed the English Channel on a boat and sailed once on a cruise ship around the Mediterranean Sea, but rugby league has proved to be my global adventure.

Not only did I journey worldwide but, throughout my years spent as a teacher, I hope that I helped to broaden the horizons of my pupils while at the same time advancing their skills and occasionally those of their hosts, as rugby players both in league and in union. Sadly, the draconian rules of the then supposedly amateur rugby union code and the persistent attention paid to my coaching of both the Lancashire Schoolboys and my first rugby club St Helens RUFC, resulted in me being banned for having played rugby league. But, thanks to the loyalty of the Lancashire schools teachers, the legal support of a rugby loving ex-pupil of mine and a briefing by Queen's Counsel gratis, I eventually overturned the ruling in regard to any participation with schoolboy rugby. Having enjoyed five years in a coaching capacity with my union club, I resigned my position rather than embarrass the club with any fight in the courts. I was more than happy to learn from Maurice Oldroyd of the British Amateur Rugby League Association that my predicament and resultant action proved to be: 'A super catalyst in the controversial issue of a free gangway between the two codes at amateur level.' Indeed, within eighteen months, that free gangway was conceded at amateur levels by the Rugby Football Union and the fifteen-a-side code was soon, at least in the Northern Hemisphere, to be dragged kicking and screaming into the real world which demanded that anyone be allowed to play any code of rugby at any time alongside and against anyone, for payment or not.

Payment for my services was never an issue as far as my

interest in schools rugby was concerned, such was the satisfaction and enjoyment I received from working with young lads and my staff colleagues. So too was the pleasure gained from helping the players at my former club to develop and improve their rugby prowess and from being able to encourage former pupils like Bath RU's John Horton, Waterloo's Dave Carfoot, David Gullick of Orrell and Widnes RL's Mick Burke to gain national and international recognition. In addition, Barrow RL's Ian Ball and Steve Tickle went on to become the gifted players they were at Craven Park. In truth, my total involvement in schoolboy rugby union and rugby league, firstly at Fairfield School in Widnes and secondly for thirty years at Cowley, led to the one great regret in my life, one which still troubles me today and constantly causes me to sigh when I ponder on what might have been.

I take great pride in having been involved in every aspect of rugby union as a player, coach, selector, administrator and, for the past ten years, the president of the St Helens RU club. I take even greater pride in my involvement in league as a player, newspaper reporter, columnist and both a radio and TV commentator and correspondent for the BBC. Yet I never tried my hand at the one job I would have loved to have sampled, coach of a major professional rugby league club and it was my own fault. In the Seventies, I was twice approached by the directors of my former club St Helens with a view to taking up the coaching role at Knowsley Road and, at my home barely a mile away from the ground, I agonised for hours with the chairman and a couple of his colleagues before coming to my decision. In January 1978, I also received a visit from a Salford deputation and was most impressed with what plans they had for the future of the Reds if I would join them. Again I declined but only after putting myself on the rack for over forty-eight hours before choosing to continue with my teaching career and, in particular, with my obsession of coaching rugby to young lads.

I have often tried to explain or understand why I refused to accept the offers of two of the biggest clubs in the game and I must confess that, even to many of my closest friends, my reasons might appear somewhat slight. Though I had some concerns that the time and attention needed to be given to any coaching job with a professional club might have an impact on my career in teaching it was, daft as it might seem to some, my loyalty to my school, pupils, their parents and my colleagues working alongside me which motivated me to continue solely with my school activities. The sheer pleasure and satisfaction I gained from working with youngsters and the companionship from grafting alongside staff of similar persuasions and inclinations made it very difficult to loosen the ties on a Saturday afternoon with schoolboy rugby.

Despite spending many hours voluntarily serving both codes, I have always been as competitive as anyone in my attitudes to winning while also believing that rugby is, whatever the outcome, only a game. Long after the score is forgotten the friends made, camaraderie, laughter and thrills of achieving something you desire are best remembered. Such was the basis of my decision, rightly or wrongly, to walk away from my ambitions of coaching a professional rugby league club. With hindsight, in the light of my media career over the past thirty-five years, it would appear that I did make the right choice. When I recall the friendships made and the laughter realised both at home and abroad while immersed in schoolboy rugby, I know I took the right decision. Especially when I remember some of the hilarious antics I and my staff were involved in, trying to raise funds to promote the game and the school's numerous tours abroad.

Throughout my involvement in rugby league, I have always been the first to raise the flag in support of international expansion and competition and ever sought to counteract the arguments that we should continue to chuck money at all grassroots developments and even clubs which have, quite simply, gone way past their sell by date and which contribute little to the overall health and impact of the sport. We have many ailing areas and clubs in our game which, by virtue of their strategic position and significance in the code, demand our support but some do not. I would ask anyone to walk down their high street and note whether any shop which was trading in 1895 (the date of the breakaway from the Rugby Football Union) is still doing so today and selling the same goods in the window. Highly unlikely and, if they still are in business, it is likely that the shop has been taken over by or merged with another bigger and more affluent concern. It is certain that such a shop will have modernised and be selling and marketing goods which are relevant to the potential customers of the day. The blinkered parochialism and over indulgence in the mythical, stereotyped northern superiority by a minority within our game hinders its development and such reactionaries must be booted into the twenty-first century. Such passionate but misguided supporters of rugby league need to be shown that any sport must have national and international exposure and involve itself heavily in international development and competition if it is to be accepted as one of the major sports in any country's portfolio.

Such an attitude must also be adopted when in charge of schoolboys, schoolgirls or youth rugby if a coach or their school or club wishes to maximise their potential. It is of little value having youngsters boasting that they are the 'cock of the walk' in their locality and believing that they are better players than they actually are when they are completely untried against opposition further afield. I firmly believe that to advance the skills and especially the attitudes of any rugby playing youngsters, no matter how successful they are, you must take them to an area outside their normal environment to show them that they can and often will be beaten and to prove that they still have much to learn. I also strongly believe that the strong must encourage the weak for only by development outside the immediate locality will any game become stronger and achieve the recognition it genuinely deserves.

In 1965, I helped to organise Cowley School's first rugby tour for eighteen lads in two mini buses - a weekend playing against Bradford Grammar School and Roundhay School in Leeds. By 1995,when I took early retirement from teaching, the school's rugby teams, in both league and union, at all age levels had travelled all over Great Britain, playing matches and competing in seven-a-side tournaments. Over the thirty years, the school's staff, parents, pupils and friends raised sufficient funds to send teams to Ireland, France, Holland and Portugal and for squads of thirty-plus boys to embark on major five and six week tours of South America, Canada, Australia and South Africa. The players' exposure to such adventures and opposition enhanced their abilities and showed them just what they had to do to attain the attitude and temperament to reach the top in either code of rugby. They helped to extend rugby's horizons and encouraged others less fortunate than themselves to develop in whatever code they played. Above all, whether raising funds to support such exotic trips or playing in Buenos Aires, Montevideo, Toronto, Sydney, Townsville, Pretoria or Port Elizabeth, they enjoyed themselves and were all the better equipped after experiencing all the drama and excitement of an overseas trip. Oh yes, there was plenty of drama and excitement but there was plenty of laughter too.

In my playing days and since, I have been privileged to be introduced to many famous personalities and have always welcomed the traditional line-up and handshake with any civic dignitaries or even royalty before a match. But never have I been as nervous or wary as when stood to be introduced to President Bordaberry of Uruguay before my Cowley School team played against his son's school in Montevideo in the summer of 1972. Having initially been greeted to the country by body searches from the gun-toting Uruguayan police and army, I was prepared for some upsets to our itinerary. Little did I realise what precautions would be taken by the authorities to protect us and especially the country's president and his son from the violent tactics of the Tupamaros Guerrillas, an urban guerrilla group who were terrorising many in high office and government. When our school party arrived at the ground of our opponents, the British School of Montevideo, the sight of four light trucks, fitted out with machine guns on the back and carrying half a dozen soldiers, circling around a specially created road surrounding the school was a little unnerving. Even more so, as I took to the field for a warm up with the school team, was the sight of supposed gardeners, hedge cutters and road sweepers going about their work with a machine gun or a rifle poking out from beneath their coat or jacket. After noting such sights, you can imagine my concern and state of mind when I drew the short straw and was designated by my other three staff colleagues as being the right man to line up before kick-off and shake hands with the President who had arrived to watch his son play in the second row for the British School.

I have lined up at Wembley Stadium before a Challenge Cup Final and shaken hands with Prime Minister Harold Wilson and Lord Derby. I have stood in the lead-up to matches and faced the likes of renowned hard men, Artie

Beetson, Brian McTigue and Derek 'Rocky' Turner. But I have never been as nervous as when I met President Bordaberry and spent eighty minutes on the touchline watching his son play against Cowley. As we shook hands, El Presidente was surrounded by armed guards and a helicopter hovered overhead containing more fierce-looking gunslingers. Nor was there any relief during the match, for wherever his son was on the pitch, whether leaping in a line out or pushing in a scrum, the helicopter followed him and circled above. I have never been as relieved to hear the final whistle in any game.

Perhaps the greatest satisfaction when making our many school trips abroad was helping to play a part in the development of other youngsters not so fortunate as those here in England. That was never more so than when, in 1993, I organised a tour of South Africa uniquely playing schools at both rugby league and rugby union. Though the matches played and the wins gained were perhaps the most important highlights to the twenty three lads who accompanied me and the other staff on the month long trip, the introduction and furtherance of rugby league in Johannesburg and our visits to Kagiso, a black township on the edge of the city, to coach the many disadvantaged youngsters proved the highlights of the tour for me.

The match between Cowley and a Johannesburg Select XIII, watched by representatives from the RFL's executive committee led by chairman Maurice Lindsay, was enthusiastically welcomed and appreciated by all who were present. But when I picture the scene of another pitch - a deserted field, almost barren of grass save for the occasional patch of brown, dead winter coverings, large stones scattered haphazardly around its perimeter and flanked by makeshift wooden terracing - my heart beats a little faster. It certainly beat faster when our collection of cars and a

'Bakki', a small open-topped truck, disgorged twenty-seven white, pink and brown pupils and staff beneath a hot sun and blue sky. We were in Kagiso but no one was around.

That is until, suddenly, small and large black figures began to emerge from out of the shanty houses, bushes and from behind the trees. With smiles on their faces, scores of young boys, aged six to nineteen were running towards us, all eager for their daily couple of hours of rugby league. How they and their school staff relished the afternoon's drills and the mini rugby matches alongside my own pupils. Their appetite for league was infectious and they certainly kept their South African coaches, Wales boss Clive Griffiths, my school staff and myself fully occupied throughout the day. Clutching photographs of the Great Britain team, and especially pictures of Ellery Hanley and Martin Offiah, they reluctantly trooped home afterwards eager for their next training session. Other pupils were equally as keen when we visited Witkoppen and Paradise Bend. Such visits were rewarding for both the South Africans and ourselves and activities with the disadvantaged youngsters gave me one more reason to think that I had been right to refrain from accepting any club coaching offers.

Such trips abroad were full of excitement and adventure for both staff and pupils but there was even more drama and laughter for all during the fundraising. When in charge of lively lads between the ages of eleven and nineteen, a teacher learns to expect anything but never did I consider some of the situations and meeting the characters I did while organising a series of annual gala days to raise funds to support rugby in the school. Whether organising a Donkey Derby or entertaining 'The World's Strongest Man', who had to be transported to hospital to receive thirty stitches after welcoming anyone to hit a large slab of concrete balanced on his head with a huge sledgehammer, a gala day can prove to be a stressful occasion. You even wonder just what you are doing when you watch a tiny, thin man, billed as the 'Human Mole', tunnel under and bury himself for hours in your school's long jump sand pit and then invite the public to win a prize by taking part in a human treasure hunt and placing a marker where he will eventually emerge - all for ten pounds cash in hand for the mole.

The auctioning of young racing pigeons donated by some of the country's leading breeders or the collecting of over a hundred tons of waste paper to raise further funds, were par for the course for any would be rugby tourist. But even I never imagined just what an uproar and excitement would be caused when, after consultation with my friend and local pet shop owner Wally Ashcroft, I decided to boost funds for a school rugby visit to Australia by holding a raffle for a live alligator. The media attention both nationally and locally in the newspapers was immense and bordered on the sensational to such an extent that I was urged by a nervous headmaster to make sure that we were insured for staging such a seemingly dangerous raffle. Stories of a wild alligator being kept in a school cupboard and carried home from school by an eleven-year-old prize winner on the local bus, all made for good publicity and the prospect of a sizeable profit on the raffle.

Thousands flocked around the school grounds on the day of the gala and, alongside an RSPCA inspector who queried the safekeeping of the exotic reptile, a large queue formed outside a classroom which displayed a big poster advising: 'Danger - Wild Alligator Inside'. An hour before the official opening of the gala, a two-ton Hertz rental truck left Wally Ashcroft's pet shop and made its way slowly from the town centre before arriving at Cowley School. The large yellow truck was backed flush to the door in the outer school wall and, to the accompaniment of loud bangings and screams from inside the body of the truck, a large container was carried inside. Tension mounted, the RSPCA inspector prepared his notebook, my headmaster checked the insurance documents and the first visitors entered the darkened classroom and stared hard at a two-foot aquarium tank placed on a table. At the side of the tank was a large magnifying glass through which to view our star prize - a two-inch stick alligator.

Cries of 'It's a confidence trick, Frenchy's done us again. It's only two inches long. You can hardly see it,' were uttered by the incredulous but smiling customers. The RSPCA inspector made a hasty exit and four hours later I helped to carry the huge profits from the raffle and the gala to the night safe of the Midland Bank. An eventful attraction but, despite the inflated insurance policy, never as dangerous as the fire-eater I booked the following year who, thanks to an overdose of petrol, set fire to the stage curtains and singed the hair of many of the audience sitting in the front row of the hall.

Organising galas, reading Shakespeare or Chaucer, coaching rugby or umpiring at cricket, immersed in pastoral care or the development of slow learners, indulging in school camps or tours abroad, performing in concerts or taking an assembly, my school life was varied and enjoyable. Indeed, I was cocooned in a cosy, comfortable world of school activities which, thanks to my passionate, obsessive but oh so enjoyable interest in schoolboy rugby cut me off temporarily from any serious involvement elsewhere. In the late-Seventies and early-Eighties I was, however, thankfully jolted back into the heady world of professional rugby league by overtures from the media which I happily accepted from newspapers, radio and TV.

13

Read All About It?

KEEN supporters of rugby league are especially irritated, and rightly so, when they turn to the back of their daily newspaper to read about their favourite sport and fail to find mention of it. Alternatively, they have to be satisfied with the contents of barely half a dozen paragraphs inserted in a side column amid the seemingly endless hype and tripe of football mania. Cricket and an inordinately large number of pages devoted to rugby union are allocated to serve the needs of their faithful followers but, despite the fact that the thirteen-a-side code is now played at professional or amateur level in every county in England, the scant levels of coverage often given to rugby league in many of our national newspapers today is shameful and unwarranted.

Whatever the tiresome excuses aired by certain sports editors of national newspapers, many of whom appear content to remain ignorant of the significance and impact of rugby league, there is no logic to the fact that a match report in the northern edition of a newspaper on a Gloucester versus Northampton union encounter can often be two or even three times the length of a rugby league game between, say, Wigan Warriors and Leeds Rhinos. Although the sales of all newspapers, whether local or national, have been undermined by the advance of the internet and other technological advances in the distribution of news and gossip, the cost cutting exercises and redundancy programmes which have severely reduced the number of sports journalists employed would appear to have shown no favours to rugby league.

Gone are the days of the Forties, Fifties and Sixties, when a follower of league could turn to the sports pages of his daily rag and find the likes of Alan Cave (*Daily Herald*), Jack Bentley (*Daily Express*), Bob Pemberton (*Daily Telegraph*), Harold Mather (*Manchester Guardian*) or Joe Humphreys (*Daily Mirror*) writing passionately on the game every day of the week. Or when, for the following twenty years or more, their full-time successors like Peter Wilson (*Daily Star*), Alan Thomas (*Daily Express*), Paul Fitzpatrick (*Guardian*), John Whalley (*Daily Telegraph*), Brian Batty (*Daily Mail*), Paul Harrison (*Sun*), Arthur Brooks and later Martin Richards (*Daily Mirror*) broke the code's major stories on a daily basis to their readers. There is still a loyal, hard core of league scribes who battle tenaciously with their bosses in London but virtually all are no longer on the full-time staff and are employed on a freelance or short contractual basis meaning they have insufficient clout to alert the needs of rugby league to too many unsympathetic superiors. There are newspapers that boast of their special multi-page, pull out sports sections and yet rely on the offerings of the Press Association for their rugby league copy. So, then, it is little wonder that any features, exclusives, background comment from major personalities within the game and in-depth coverage of important issues are lacking. Many reasons are trotted out by our sports editors in answer to the complaints of the long suffering rugby league fans. The age old excuse of league being 'only a northern game' will invariably still be at the forefront, while the limited international competition of recent years will also be cited as restricting the exposure of the game in the nationals. But the demise of the newspapers' own print industry in Manchester and the departure from the city of the large, fully-staffed offices between 1985 and '95, once on parity with those in London, has surely been the major reason for any perceived lack of worthwhile rugby league content. The departure from Manchester of senior editorial input, major news gathering or writing and mass printing meant that, once all had been transferred to London and staff had been declared redundant, thanks to the introduction of modern technology, there was not the same consciousness of the significance and importance of rugby league in the south.

Whatever the impact of local newspapers and radio on the promotion of sport for the past quarter of a century, London has been central to extensive media exposure for any game, be it football, cricket, hockey, rugby union or league. It is not bias against a sport which governs the attention given to it but rather an ignorance of the sport itself and its relevance to the wider public by those in charge of the content of our daily newspapers. A former long serving RL journalist, who experienced the heady days of the once great Manchester newspaper offices and also their disappearance, aptly summed up his experiences when he eventually came to be providing daily copy on the sport for his superiors in London. As he insists: 'When I spoke to my bosses in London about the rugby league coverage for the day I suddenly felt like the opening batsman in a cricket Test match. The people bowling the bouncers and the beamers at me however were the fast bowlers in my own side.'

The impending move by the Sports Department of BBC TV and also that of BBC Radio Five Live to Salford will, I believe, have a dramatic impact on the coverage of rugby league and help to persuade the sports editors of our daily newspapers to increase their output. Television today leads sports coverage and the newspapers, though still quite rightly proud of their exclusive stories and their own personal comment, have to take note of and follow what is being promoted on the major sports broadcasting organisations. Television, more than at any time in its history, sets the agenda for sport and, by its extensive funding, ensures the very existence of most major sports. TV and radio producers, editors, researchers and correspondents living and working in and around Salford and the north west will have a consciousness for rugby league whether they are merely overhearing conversation about the game in their local pub, restaurant, supermarket, on the bus or the train. They will be confronting the game whenever they open their local weekly or evening newspapers and see copies of *League Weekly* and *League Express*, the weekly trade papers, on the counters at their local newsagents. Whether they are a supporter or not, there will be an appetite for and awareness of rugby league and that must play its part surely in ensuring that the game receives its true deserts. It is highly significant that the Rugby Football League is considering moving a section of their media/marketing department to Salford or Manchester when the huge BBC TV and Radio Media City finally arrives up north.

Ironically, although the period from the mid-Eighties to mid-Nineties proved a troublesome time for many involved in newspapers, the new technology adopted by such entrepreneurs as Eddie Shah, the owner of *Today*, brought about my own introduction to the world of rugby league journalism. Having been asked by the publication to become their rugby league correspondent, I enjoyed ten years reporting and commenting on the game until the tabloid was bought and eventually closed down by Rupert Murdoch. Under the guidance of my sports bosses Mike Crouch and Geoff Sweet, both of whom were sympathetic to rugby league, I was given free reign to report on the game and allowed to wander wherever my pen and note book took me. That even extended to the Southern Hemisphere and the islands of Papua New Guinea and Fiji and all the drama, excitement and fun which surrounds the playing of the sport in such exotic countries.

How well I recall some of the matches played in PNG and the mayhem, chaos and even danger which often surrounded a fiercely contested match when the local team's passionate and highly excitable supporters were aroused. On one tour in 1990, many of the visiting Great Britain players and the media had commemorative T-shirts made with the words 'Tear Gas Tour' printed on the front.

Papua New Guinea is a beautiful country, its people in the main are friendly and generous but in the outlying rugby regions of Lae, Goroka or in Rabaul, a small township on the island of New Britain off the coast, I found that - such was their fervour - there was always the potential of an explosive situation at any ground. Possible outbursts of temper or passion were not evident when our touring party arrived by plane at the tiny town of Goroka, nestling almost six thousand feet up in the beautiful Highlands. Magnificent scenery all around, towering peaks, brilliantly coloured birds of paradise flying on high, the yellows, reds and pinks of the flowering trees and a motley crew of half-naked dancers greeted us as we descended from the plane. Hundreds of wildly cheering and singing natives led and followed our walk down the main street to our hotel and many wearing ceremonial head dresses and painted from head to toe in brilliant red, yellow and blue ochres, remained outside the building all night before converging on the ground the next day. Having often walked for many miles through dense undergrowth, whole families packed into the small stadium while those locked outside climbed the many trees surrounding it to gain any vantage point. Anticipation for the clash with Great Britain was so high that tempers became almost uncontrollable when the referee's whistle intervened too frequently against the home side or a decision cost the local team a win.

Gunfire and exploding tear gas canisters accompanied Great Britain's controversial opening 20-18 Test defeat against Papua New Guinea in that intimidating Goroka atmosphere in 1990. Armed police struggled to control hundreds of stone throwing fans locked outside the stadium and, as the disturbances grew worse with Great Britain leading, there were rapid rifle volleys as police fired over the heads of the rioters and tear gas canisters were thrown in an attempt to quell the local's ardour. Some landed inside the ground and, when the gas drifted slowly across the pitch a number of the Great Britain players were forced to run to escape it. Problems too in the press box, where several reporters including myself were affected by the tear gas and could hardly focus our eyes on the action when the match was eventually resumed.

By far the worst example of how easily a friendly and welcoming people can be aroused by an over intense passion for their sport was to be seen in the once beautiful town of Rabaul, now sadly destroyed by falling ash from a volcanic eruption in 1994. Just twenty-three minutes into the match between the Islands Zone and Great Britain, hundreds of frightened fans tore down the fences surrounding the picturesque Queen Elizabeth Stadium to escape from the stinging tear gas which had been used to stop them trying to break into the packed ground. Great Britain coach Mal Reilly, tears streaming from his eyes, ushered his players to the side of the pitch where they were placed under police guard for a quarter of an hour. The players huddled together coughing and spluttering, clutching their throats and sucking ice cubes to relieve the burning sensation in their mouths. A policeman who threw the first gas canister and even the unfortunate referee, after the match, were held temporarily in the local police cells. Chaos, excitement and a little 'black magic' too was not unheard of whenever a match needed to be won by the Islands.

Visitors to Papua New Guinea on any Sunday morning will regularly have their ears regaled by the singing from the many packed churches, often with worshippers overflowing into the streets. But there is also a curious mix of beliefs and traditions on the islands representing religion and superstition. Hence my dramatic but hilarious meeting with a practising witch doctor who sent the then rugby league correspondent for the *Sun*, Paul Harrison and myself fearfully racing back to our hotel as fast as our legs could carry us.

On hearing that the Zone's players had called in a local witch doctor for his help in defeating the touring Lions' team and, indeed, had cast a spell on the Great Britain XIII, Paul and I ventured into the dense forestry to meet him and record his tale for our respective newspapers. Aided and driven in a car by our guide Michael, the barman from our hotel, we left the highway, skirted around the Japanese War Bunker frequented by Vice Admiral Kusaka in the 1939-45 Pacific campaigns and entered the dense undergrowth which surrounded the village of Raluana. There, sitting under a coconut tree and clad in his native lap lap skirt was an old gentleman, tipping the scales at about seventeen or eighteen stone, ready to greet us. Surrounded by coconut palms, bananas, dried leaves and pots and pans, he welcomed us both with a huge smile and a shake of the hand.

Unfortunately, the greeting faded when he learned from our guide the purpose of our mission. He misunderstood the message, believing that we had come to steal his secrets and magic spells. His smile suddenly disappeared and was replaced by a huge scowl. A low rumbling cry erupted from somewhere in his large stomach and from between his lips. He angrily turned his back and, before a large, thick cane descended upon our heads, Michael our frightened guide, insisted we beat a hasty retreat through the coconut groves and the swaying palms. A shocked and trembling Michael drove us at great speed back to our hotel, explaining to us that the witch doctor had also put a curse on us and that he would have to return later to beg the old gentleman to relieve us of the spell.

Though never learning of his secrets, our guide did explain how, in an effort to defeat the Lions, the Islands Zone players had consulted the witch doctor as a motivational aid. An overnight stay in the bush, a potion of liquids and a rub down in coconut oil for all the team members was supposed to cause havoc in the British camp and give an inner strength to the recipients. Unusual tactics when compared to the motivational blasts once used by former international coaches Alex Murphy or Peter Fox but then perfectly normal in Rabaul where, alongside the many white, bright timbered churches, the influence of the village witch doctor was still strong. Sadly for the local practitioner we visited, his lotions, potions and spell were obviously not powerful enough. Great Britain beat the Islands Zone in a ten-try romp by fifty points to four.

More stress and strain off the pitch too when I visited the Patel Stadium in Nadi, Fiji, prior to Great Britain's tour of New Zealand in 1996 to report on the clash between the home nation and the Lions. No worries surrounding the match reports or the broadcast for BBC Radio but I was seriously embarrassed when trying to drink the local Kava brew with the country's genial President before the kick-off. Kava, a brown bitter herbal drink, is often imbibed in the Pacific at ceremonies or meetings to honour visitors and unite guests and their hosts. Today it is considered by many medical practitioners to be soothing, its ingredients having the effect of calming one's nerves and easing stress. The lukewarm substance, served in a huge round bowl and offered to me, certainly had the opposite effect. I couldn't stomach the taste and, throughout my meeting and discussions with the President and his entourage, I was constantly pouring the kava onto the roots of a bush behind me. Hopefully he never took offence or realised what I was doing with his country's traditional offering.

International stars Stanley Gene, Bal Numapo, Adrian Lam, Petero Civoniceva, Jarryd Hayne and Noa Nadruku are but a handful of players who have highlighted the calibre produced in Papua New Guinea and Fiji. The Papuans, by nature, are somewhat small in stature but they are also extremely tough, combative players, genuine hard men who never take a backwards step. And they are crafty footballers, always looking to play fast, attacking rugby league. The Fijians, renowned for their handling and running skills in rugby union when playing the sevens variety especially, are big men who relish the open running of league and sheer physicality of the one-on-one tackling. Little wonder that many are now finding their way into the ranks of the engage Super League and Co-operative Championship in Great Britain and in the National Rugby

League in Australia and New Zealand. The abilities of Leeds Rhino Ali Lauitiiti, George Carmont of Wigan and St Helens pair Francis Meli and Maurie Fa'asavalu are but four examples of the powerful players currently joining the ranks from Samoa, while the likes of George Mann, Emosi Koloto, Tevita Vaikona and the former Wigan stars Kevin and Tony Iro helped to kick start the production line of players today trying their hand at rugby league from Tonga and the Cook Islands. There is no doubt that as well as being exciting and rewarding to visit such hospitable nations, it is evident that the Pacific Island players are ideally suited to playing rugby league and that all of the emerging countries are making a serious contribution to the strength and attraction of the sport, not only at club level but, significantly, internationally as well. That was there for all to see in the outstanding performances of Papua New Guinea and Fiji in the last World Cup held Down Under in 2008. The recently introduced play-off system between Papua New Guinea, Samoa, Fiji, the Cook Islands and Tonga to decide the Pacific nation to compete in the bi-annual Four Nations Tournament alongside Great Britain, New Zealand and Australia, beginning in 2010, can only help the further emergence of talented players.

The Pacific Islands can provide any visitor with pleasant shocks but we should not be surprised at the depth and wealth of the talent now emerging from such exotic nations, for the players' mental approach, attitude and their physical strength are ideal characteristics for success in rugby league. They and the game as a whole will prosper if we continue to provide such natural performers and their homelands with a pathway to the top in the code. Such outstanding overseas players have frequently entertained me, the fans and TV viewers worldwide, despite the fact that occasionally the pronunciation of their names has caused me a minor headache when behind the microphone sitting in the commentary box for BBC TV.

After a gentle introduction to the world of television as a summariser, I was stunned and shocked to be asked to take over the role of rugby league commentator for BBC TV from my inimitable predecessor, Eddie Waring.

It was a total surprise when, at a book launch in 1979, I was approached by Keith Phillips, then a BBC sports producer based in Manchester and, along with his counterpart in London, Nick Hunter, heavily involved in the broadcasting of rugby league. I was not expecting his invitation to sit alongside Eddie Waring in the commentary box but I gladly accepted the offer and duly reported for duty at Lawkholme Lane, now Cougar Park, home of Keighley for their BBC Two Floodlit Trophy match against Hull Kingston Rovers. Though I knew Eddie quite well from my playing days, I was nervous and curious as to how I would be received by him and fascinated to learn how he went about broadcasting a commentary. He welcomed me instantly and warmly before kick-off and, having unfurled a huge list of the names of both teams with notes alongside each individual player, he placed it on a desk in front of him. He then put a small bag of sliced fruit - oranges, pineapple, grapefruit and apple - alongside the large sheet of white card and proceeded to eat the fruit at intervals during the match in order to keep his mouth moist. An assistant, Norman Graveson, was on hand to offer some help in recognising the players by occasionally pointing at their name on the sheet if Eddie was uncertain who was in possession of the ball or had scored.

Fascinated by Eddie's mannerisms and methods, I took little interest in the game itself, only being used in the commentary to describe and talk over every replayed try that he had described live. I soon learned that a summariser had to be brief and concise with his words or, as I was, constantly caught out by the lack of time available for his offerings. But, as Eddie mixed his comments with a bite from an apple slice or a suck on a grapefruit segment, I began to enjoy the experience alongside him. Little did I realise or even dare to hope that, after another dozen or so appearances alongside him over the next fifteen months, I would follow in his footsteps and, like him, have the honour and pleasure of becoming a part of BBC TV's long and unique association with rugby league. I should however have realised there was to be a vacancy when, at the end of the 1980/81 season, it took both of us ten minutes to climb to the TV gantry to our commentary box via a thin, insecure, metal rung ladder attached to the back of the stand at the Boulevard, Hull with an out of breath Eddie insisting profusely that it was, 'time to call it a day.'

14

Into the Hotseat

THE sweet and sour king prawns which followed my starter of crispy spring rolls was proving the perfect choice as I relaxed at midnight one Saturday evening in the summer of 1981 in the Flower Drum, a highly recommended Chinese restaurant in Melbourne, Australia. Along with my teaching colleagues from Cowley School and half a dozen staff from Melbourne Grammar School, I was celebrating our touring team's win over the local opposition during the afternoon.

Suddenly, a small Chinese waiter interrupted our celebrations by asking our group if there was a 'Mr Lay Flench' dining at the table. 'Mr Lay Flench, is there a Mr Lay Flench at the table? Mr Lay Flench is wanted on the telephone,' he insisted. Tucking into my tasty dish and making sure that I didn't miss out on the extra portions of rice which were being handed around I replied: 'No, there is no Lay Flench here. We are from England.'

'Yes, Mr Lay Flench from England. He is wanted on the telephone from England. It is urgent.'

'Do you mean Ray French?' I asked.

'Yes,' he replied.

Whenever I have been in charge of any school tour to foreign parts, a telephone call late at night usually signified disturbing news, a problem at home for a member of staff or pupil, the cancellation of a bus, train or ship due to move our party elsewhere the next day, or instruction that my front row were spending a night in the local police cells. All manner of thoughts rushed through my head as I followed the waiter to the restaurant's reception desk and took hold of the telephone. When the very English voice twelve thousand miles away at the end of the line asked, 'Is that Ray French?' and proceeded to inquire if I would like to take over from Eddie Waring as the voice of rugby league for BBC TV, I sensed that I was being set up by my school team captain who had a sense of humour for such escapades. Casting aside the dignity of my normal schoolmasterly approach, I replied in blunt, simple terms: 'Piss off!'

Thankfully the speaker on the other end took little heed of my advice and continued to ask me if I did wish to fill Eddie's role and, if I did, could he announce the decision to the media. About to offer another profanity to the caller, I became aware that all was not right with my responses to his requests when, in the background, I heard the faint sound of a cricket commentary. On hearing the disembodied voice describing the state of the wicket, I instantly changed tone and mellowed my language, a tactic which quickly enabled me to learn that the caller was Nick Hunter, then in charge of BBC TV's production of rugby league and that his first question to me regarding my future employment was indeed a genuine one. Apology after apology followed when I learned that, alongside producing the cricket from Old Trafford, he had spent an hour trying to track me down in Australia by first telephoning my wife, Helen, as to my whereabouts, the headmaster of the Melbourne Grammar School, the wife of the master in charge of rugby at the school and about six Chinese restaurants in downtown Melbourne before finally getting Mr Lay Flench in the Flower Drum.

Thankfully Nick Hunter laughed off my initial reply to his request and, with the offer of a starting twelve months contract, invited me once again to join him at BBC TV Sport as the terrestrial station's rugby league commentator. Though I had been engaged in match commentating and reporting for BBC Radio Merseyside for a number of years, my latest shock appointment filled me with awe for the responsibility invested in me both by the Corporation and the game. It might seem trite in today's all too cynical world but I was honoured and still am proud to be a part of the BBC's long association with the game and despite whatever criticism, rightly or wrongly, hurled at it over the years, its unique and unswerving support for the sport.

The first indication of the BBC's coverage of rugby league could be seen by all the readers of the *Radio Times* in 1927, when it was announced that a Mr Ernest Blackwell would commentate live on radio during the Challenge Cup final between Oldham and Swinton at Central Park, Wigan. The BBC's weekly publication featured a plan of the pitch divided into eight numbered areas, in an effort to enable listeners to know where play was taking place during the broadcast. For the next thirty years, until full national radio coverage of the Challenge Cup was introduced permanently, the contest was aired on regional or national radio depending on the inclinations of each region. Interestingly for the 1938 and 1939 deciders, the BBC introduced the practice of having different commentators in each half of the match, the first for northern listeners and the second for the national commentary.

The BBC has continued to broadcast the Challenge Cup final on radio - and eventually other club and international matches - for the past eighty-three years and today the game receives extensive news coverage and full match commentaries of virtually every professional match on a weekly basis via BBC local radio, the BBC's internet services and BBC Radio Five Live and Five Live Sports Extra. BBC radio naturally proved a vital asset in the code's attempts to widen its influence and impact nationwide but it was television, and especially BBC TV's unbroken coverage and involvement with the game since 1958, which introduced it to every household in Britain and many abroad. Such exposure has enabled the Rugby Football League to gather in much needed income from TV fees, sponsorship and advertising.

Joe Egan and Ernest Ward, the captains of Wigan and Bradford Northern, were the first to lead out their teams before BBC TV's cameras in the 1948 Challenge Cup Final at Wembley Stadium, although the former England and Lancashire cricketer George Duckworth's and Michael Henderson's live commentary of the game was only transmitted in the London region. The following two Cup Finals were also aired throughout the midlands regions and it was season 1951/52 which heralded the first major breakthrough for rugby league in its association with television. The introduction into the network of the Holme Moss transmitter on the top of the Pennines allowed television to be seen in the north of England and there were many, including myself, my dad and granddad, who crowded around a nine-inch Bush screen at home or in shops on the high street to watch, for the first time, rugby league live on TV. The opening Test between Great Britain and New Zealand, the league match pitting Wigan and Wakefield Trinity and the 1952 Challenge Cup Final which saw Featherstone Rovers clash with Workington Town were all shown live nationwide. Despite the clash between Keighley and the Australian touring team being shown live nationally on BBC TV from Lawkholme Lane at the beginning of the 1952/53 season, sadly the effects of such broadcasts on the attendances were believed to be such that the Rugby League Council refused to allow any further coverage of the Challenge Cup climax until 1958.Thankfully, good sense finally prevailed at League headquarters and normal service was resumed by the BBC with my predecessor Eddie Waring and the RFL's own secretary, Bill Fallowfield at the microphones. Eddie, also occasionally accompanied by David Watkins or Alex Murphy, took the lead in every Challenge Cup Final until 1981 when I had the privilege of taking over from him. Via the BBC's *Grandstand* programme, he introduced a nationwide audience to over thirty matches a season including league, cup, Test and World Cup fixtures.

ITV, apart from an early partnership with rugby league in a series of floodlit matches, a seven-a-side tournament in London in the early Fifties and Sixties and, in 1965, the broadcasting of amateur inter-town under-17s and 19s matches on a Sunday afternoon, has shown little interest in providing any continuous coverage. Of real benefit has been the arrival on our screens of Sky, a company which, thanks to its many sports-dedicated channels, can allocate a considerable amount of its output and money to the benefit of rugby league. As with football, cricket, rugby union and other major sports in this country, Sky TV's huge financial resources help to underpin the salary cap structure and funding of the game. However, although their rugby league coverage is both innovative and expansive the limited viewing nature of satellite television means that the terrestrial BBC still remains the vital, vibrant outlet for attracting millions of viewers and influential sponsors and backers to the delights of the game.

But for the promptings of a couple of friends, I would never have applied for the role of rugby league commentator for BBC TV. Such were the number of names being bandied about as possible successors to Eddie in the gossip columns of the Sunday newspapers I believed that I would have little chance of success. My good friend Keith Macklin, who was working with ITV at the time and John Helm, who later assumed the role of soccer commentator for Yorkshire TV, were reported as being front runners for the job. Former Great Britain and Salford winger Keith Fielding and ex Wales RU and RL star David Watkins, both of whom had worked alongside Eddie as summarisers, were also believed to be among the four hundred-plus applicants. No matter, I duly mentioned to Keith Phillips, one of the BBC's rugby league producers, that I would like to be considered for the post and waited patiently until, along with another forty would-be commentators, I was invited to the BBC TV sports studios in Manchester to record a forty minute demonstration tape on the second half of a pre-recorded Championship Final. Once my ordeal was over, I was so immersed in my school duties and raising funds for the rugby team's five-week trip to Australia that I completely forgot about BBC and rugby league. That is until that fateful night in the Flower Drum Restaurant in Melbourne and my rather blunt reply to Keith's colleague and co-producer.

How or why I was ever chosen to be the voice of rugby league for BBC TV I have never been told but I understand that the former Wales and British Lions RU half-back star Cliff Morgan, then the Head of BBC Sport, gave me his backing. Throughout my early years with the BBC he was a great support to me, often visiting me on the TV gantry before kick-off to a Challenge Cup Final or offering sound words of advice. I well recall his words when he invited me to a lunch in Manchester shortly before my first commentary. 'If fifty per cent love you and fifty per cent hate you, then you will be doing a good job. If a hundred per cent love you or a hundred per cent hate you, then you have a problem.' It is a criterion for success which, after reading the many letters of praise or complaint occasionally sent to the TV Centre at White City concerning my match commentaries, I am convinced I more than fulfilled.

Many missives forwarded to me from places as distant as Kilkee in Ireland, Aberdeen in Scotland, Neath in Wales or Padstow in Cornwall are from people adding to an anecdote or reference made to a person or an incident in a match. Writers less acquainted with rugby league will often ask for clarification on a rule or a tactical matter while the aficionados of the game will often counter an argument or a point made by myself or the summariser during a match. A few letters, apart from their obvious sincerity, are amusing and ones which I cherish.

Having defeated Bradford Bulls in the 1996 Challenge Cup Final, St Helens were heavily beaten by their Cup opponents when they made their next visit to the Odsal Stadium. The following letter was forwarded to me from an irate Bradford supporter.

> Dear sir,
> Unfortunately I was unable to attend the clash between the Bradford Bulls and St Helens but was delighted to be able to purchase a video of the match which highlighted a tremendous win by the Bulls over the Cup winners, St Helens. You'd expect some supportive comment from ex -Saints forward, Ray French, but I'm afraid that my video has been ruined by his disgraceful,

pathetic, paltry and at times laughable commentary. Some of his comments bordered on the childish like a schoolboy who'd had his lollipop stolen in the playground and only in the last five minutes, as if to make amends for his ridiculous comments, did he ever refer to what was a terrific performance by the Bulls. His biased and lamentable commentary is certainly not called for and if commentators could be called up before the Rugby League's Disciplinary Council for bringing the game into disrepute then Ray French would be a prime candidate.

I wasn't even at the match as I was commentating for BBC Radio Merseyside on a Warrington versus Castleford game on the same day! The match broadcast was in fact done by a good friend of mine, Ron Hoofe, who in a somewhat similar St Helens accent provides commentaries for local consumption on all Saints matches for sale in the club shop.

A second letter from Hemel Hempstead illustrates how any commentator needs to do his research before a match, especially when, like me, he has given undue praise to Leeds' Australian centre Tony Currie for his immaculate catching and handling in atrocious wet and rainy conditions in a clash against Hull at the Boulevard.

Dear French,
Last Saturday I overheard your comments regarding the surprisingly good handling of the Leeds Australian centre, Tony Currie, in the wet weather. Are you not aware that the average rainfall in Sydney can often be higher than that of Hull while in the surrounding area of the

Australian city it can often be much higher? In the week specifically referred to in your commentary the water levels have occasionally risen well above those of Hull.

There is no excuse whatever for such gross inaccuracy in your commentaries. If ever you wish to make an impact as a commentator you really must indulge yourself in far greater research than you apparently do at the moment. I have forwarded the water level tables for New South Wales.

Disgusted,
Hemel Hempstead

PS. If I must be honest you are bloody hopeless.

With accompanying apologies for the vocabulary used, a third letter admirably sums up the passions of a rugby league supporter from Liverpool who, true to Scouse tradition, tells it as he sees it and succinctly too.

Dear sir,

I regularly listen to your commentaries on BBC Radio Merseyside and I see you jumping up and down in the press box at Knowsley Road. You talk a load of shite. Why don't you stick that microphone up your arse?

Yours faithfully,
A genuine RL fan

PS. My mother thinks your interviews are crap.

It is interesting to note that many of the irate letter writers often add a PS to their words of advice, in their frustration seemingly unable to contain themselves with just one attack on the unfortunate commentator.

After a dummy run and a practice commentary on the second division match between Cardiff City and Salford at Ninian Park, I tackled my first game for the BBC - the Lancashire Cup Final played between Leigh and Widnes - on Saturday 26th September, 1981 at Central Park, Wigan. While perched high in a tiny commentary box-cum-pigeon coop on top of the dilapidated, small, wooden grandstand, I learned a golden rule for commentators: never leave your match notes balanced on the edge of an open window. That is especially so on wet and windy afternoons for, within five minutes of my first national broadcast, my rain sodden notes had virtually disintegrated and were to fall and be blown onto the heads of the spectators crowded below on the terraces. Seventy-five minutes of further commentary without a single note or statistic in my first match and yet I was thankful of the experience and especially so when, some hours later, my home telephone rang with an unknown caller from Leigh simply saying: 'Tha' did well, lad.' I wonder if he would have offered his compliments had his side not won by eight points to three. My career as a TV commentator was underway but following a legendary though controversial figure like Eddie Waring was daunting and, in the first few months, I experienced the pressures of taking over from him. More so when Nick Hunter informed me that in two months' time he intended to sit down with me and discuss my progress behind the microphone.

To follow in the footsteps of a man who, apart from being the sole commentator on rugby league on BBC TV, was a co-host of one of the most popular shows on television, *It's a Knockout*, and had danced and sung on the *Morecambe and Wise Christmas Show* was almost an impossibility. Little wonder then that the BBC, though very appreciative of all that he had done, insisted that they didn't want another Eddie Waring but a Ray French, commentating in his own style and voice. Thanks to Eddie's jaunty, quirky and humorous style and his broadcasting activities away from rugby league, he had enthused many but annoyed and infuriated a minority of ardent devotees of the game who saw his approach to commentating as belittling the image of the sport. At a time when huge audiences in the winter months used to turn to BBC's *Grandstand* programme to watch their weekly diet of live sport, rugby league was one of the most accessible and hence, the most popular. I believe that Eddie, whether deliberately or accidentally, captured the mood of the wide, diverse audience and helped to popularise the game to many who were unfamiliar with it. To many who insist that his often all too light-hearted approach harmed the image of the sport, I would argue that the homely, warmth he portrayed of the game and its players only added to its appeal. A commentator must naturally project his character during a match and realise that humour, anecdotal comment and banter with a summariser or co-commentator are vital if one is speaking to viewers on a terrestrial channel like BBC TV, many of whom will know little about the intricacies of play.

Any commentator, whether he is delivering football, cricket, rugby, must be true to himself and his own character or he will soon be exposed by his audience. My rugby league colleagues on Sky Sports, Eddie Hemmings and Mike Stephenson, broadcast on a channel which, primarily, attracts dedicated sports and rugby league followers. Such is the viewing nature of satellite TV that the vast majority of their punters know all there is to know about the game, hence Eddie and Mike can often assume much and commentate accordingly. On BBC TV, faced with a large and varied terrestrial audience, many of whom know little of the rules or style of play in rugby league, I and my fellow commentator Dave Woods must, at the risk of irritating the rugby league devotee, occasionally explain a rule, highlight a defensive ploy, explain a tactic employed or offer a touch of humour to interest the casual viewers. But, above all, the commentator must tell it as he sees it in his own personal style and, whether he succeeds or fails, he must copy no one. Indeed, I would recommend that in his early days at the microphone, as I did, he listens to no other commentator so that his words, style and manner are his own. To both the half who love him and the balance who hate him, he will be instantly recognisable. My predecessor was, as was the sport when he brought it to millions sitting at home in their armchairs.

We should not forget Eddie Waring's contribution and his knowledge and love of the code. Not only did he write on the sport at home and abroad, he was a most successful manager of the Dewsbury club in the late-Thirties and during the Second World War. His ambitious 'guest' signings of some of the all-time greats of the game for the humble Yorkshire outfit during the hostilities - like Wigan's Jim Sullivan and Salford's Gus Risman - brought considerable success to Crown Flatt. His entrepreneurial flair, which was revealed later during his TV career, was also amply illustrated by his attempts to introduce and promote baseball matches at the venue between American and English teams during the war years. I was never destined to be an Eddie Waring, hopefully I was a Ray French.

For how long I was to be allowed to commentate as Ray French was to be explained to me by Nick Hunter at a meeting of the two of us over dinner at the Swan Hotel at Newby Bridge in Cumbria, on the Friday night prior to a televised clash in December '81, between Barrow and Hull. Having been informed by Nick that he would only arrive at the hotel at around 7.30pm and would go straight into dinner after checking in at reception, we arranged to meet in the foyer. Driving to Cumbria following a meeting at school,

Ray French ...And Rugby

I arrived with little time to spare and, without paying too much attention to what was happening around me, went immediately to my room to get changed for dinner. Imagine my surprise when, on leaving my room at the appointed time, I stepped into the corridor and had to allow three large ladies, carrying large baskets of fruit and dressed in 1880s style clothing, to use the lift ahead of me. Thinking that they must be hotel employees adding a little colour and atmosphere, I thought little about their presence and appearance until, at the next floor, two pirates sporting black cocked and feathered hats and wearing striped black and white vests joined us in the lift. I became even more intrigued when three more ladies clad in exotic Japanese dress greeted all of us as we left the lift on the ground floor.

Nick Hunter, wearing a normal BBC-type executive suit, was waiting to meet me at the door of the hotel's dining room with a large smile on his face.

'You'll never believe this, Ray,' he said. 'Take a look inside. We will be the only two dining in normal dress. It's the annual dinner tonight of a Gilbert and Sullivan Operatic Society, everyone's come in fancy dress from one of the operas.'

Guests acting out the roles of characters from *The Pirates of Penzance*, *HMS Pinafore*, *Ruddigore*, *The Mikado* and other operas were taking their seats around the dining tables. A small table for two was reserved for Nick and myself in the corner of the large dining room. Nick's intention to outline my progress or otherwise as a commentator during dinner was a non-starter when, immediately the soup had been served and after and during every course, the guests from each table took it in turns to accompany a pianist with a medley of songs from their favourite opera. When a table of diminutive ladies clad in kimonos, stood up and started singing, 'Three little maids from school are we, full to the brim with girlish glee....' Nick turned to me and said:

170

'Forget any debriefing, you are doing fine. Let's enjoy the soup and the singing.'

We did and I never learned what he thought about my efforts in the commentary box.

Such incidents, however, taught me always to expect the unexpected and be prepared for the most dramatic of events both on and off the pitch when commentating or reporting on rugby league, wherever that may be. Various incidents confirmed my belief that, even though the preparation for and the commentaries themselves might be classed as work by other people, to me they would always be an enjoyable and passionate hobby for which I was lucky enough to be paid a fee.

Lancashire and Yorkshire Cup matches, John Player Cup or Regal Trophy ties, Tests, Lions Tour games and World Cup tournaments stretched out in front of me like a pick and mix toffee stall ahead of a five-year-old. All the excitement, drama, spectacle and majesty of the Challenge Cup lay in wait and I was more than ready to sample those sunlit days at the Final in May or August in London, Cardiff or Edinburgh, when my hobby became an international event and my game was recognised worldwide. I felt very humble when I set out on that Saturday morning from the Swan Hotel at Newby Bridge on my way to the Craven Park ground in Barrow and the next three decades of my 'employment' with the BBC.

Oh yes and the drama started just two hours before that Regal Trophy battle between Barrow and Hull when Nick and I learned that the window of the tiny wooden shelter on the top of the rickety grandstand being used for the commentary box was of the stained glass, leaded type normally reserved for churches. A quick telephone call to a local glazier saw the window removed from the box just ten minutes before kick-off, in time to enable me to see the players and describe the action.

15

Telly Like it Is

IF I had a pound for every Aussie or Kiwi player who has told me that he and his dad used to get up in the middle of the night in Wagga Wagga or Whangerei to listen to me commentating on the rugby league Challenge Cup Final, I would be able to achieve my aim of becoming a sugar daddy to an ailing club. If I had a pound for every email which has winged its way to the studios of BBC Merseyside from internet listeners in Cologne, Wisconsin, Buenos Aires, Cape Town and elsewhere worldwide during our local radio commentaries on St Helens, Warrington, Widnes and Wigan matches, I would be able to fund two clubs. Indeed, thanks to the arrival of the internet, local radio should now be referred to as international radio such is its reach abroad.

The influence of the media on sport is now all-embracing and all-powerful. It determines the impact made by any game on the public and is crucial to its financial well-being. A sport like rugby league which is not blessed with the outrageous but rewarding hype which surrounds football and still appears not to have the social cachet which attracts the media to rugby union and cricket, is rewarded by ample and invaluable television coverage. Since the introduction of Super League in 1996, the influence of Sky TV has been immense, not only in terms of their excellent and extensive coverage of Super League, Championship, International and even student matches with the annual Oxford v Cambridge RL Varsity game, but also in terms of their features and news programmes. Their considerable financial contribution is vital to rugby league clubs' coffers. Unfortunately, for all the enthusiasm and professionalism of Sky's commentators and presenters Eddie Hemmings, Mike Stephenson, Phil Clarke and Bill Arthur, plus a host of other contributions from rugby league luminaries, notably Brian Carney, Terry O'Connor and Barrie McDermott, a satellite company does not have the viewer reach of a terrestrial organisation the size of the BBC. The extra costs incurred by any household for watching programmes by subscription can also be prohibitive to many. As a consequence, despite rugby league proving itself to be one of the most popular team sports shown on satellite and posting ever increasing viewing figures in 2010, the audiences for rugby league are far bigger and more widespread in their numbers on BBC TV. The terrestrial station, by its reach to virtually every household, pub and club in the land, offers a large catchment, not only to the devotees of the game but to general lovers of sport and even casual viewers who merely wish to be entertained for an hour or two.

Admittedly, while wearing my BBC hat (or flat cap), let me unashamedly insist that the sheer professionalism and dedication of those talented people behind the screen at BBC TV throughout the sixty-two years association between the station and our game have proved to be a key component in the progress of the code, have helped to bolster its impact during times of strife and have more than played their part in presenting the game as an entertaining attraction. That is despite the constant carping and criticism of the BBC's intentions towards rugby league which often comes, rightly or wrongly, from some disgruntled grassroots supporters. It may be that, because of the lack of rugby league content in the southern editions of our daily newspapers and the shortage of conversation about rugby league in the pubs, restaurants and on the tube and buses south of Watford, there is a lack of appreciation for the game with some who influence matters within the BBC. The reduction in the amount of rugby league now covered by BBC TV in its sport portfolio is, however, more due to the lack of funds now available and the buying up of the rights to so many tournaments and competitions by the cash-rich BSkyB. For that reason, it is especially pleasing to note that once again certain international matches are now able to be shown live by the BBC, an arrangement which, in the past, enabled the likes of Martin Offiah, Ellery Hanley, Garry Schofield and others to become household names and thereby raise the profile of both the sport and the broadcaster.

Never in my thirty-year association with BBC TV have I ever come across any favouring of union at the expense of league, nor have I met with the bias which some suggest lurks in the corridors of power at Television Centre in White City. If such accusations were to have any foundation, then I would suggest that, given the backgrounds and inclinations of BBC TV's rugby league production staff, such bias would be heavily in favour of the thirteen-a-side code. I would bet that there is no production team working on rugby league anywhere which is more immersed in its subject and part of the fabric of it. When I open my mouth on any topic relevant to the game, I have to be confident of my facts such is the knowledge and interest of the production crew. Carl Hicks, the BBC's league and union editor, is a born and bred Widnesian and a passionate supporter of the Vikings; his assistant editor Alistair McIntyre hails from an avenue just five hundred yards from Knowsley Road and is a staunch fan of the Saints. Sally Richardson, the producer of rugby league, is proud of her upbringing in Baildon, Yorkshire and supports Leeds Rhinos while the rugby league match director Ken Burton is of good Barrow stock and keeps in close touch with the happenings at Craven Park. Our renowned presenter on screen, Clare Balding is, as even the most biased of critics is aware, an ardent follower and keen admirer of everything about the sport. I am grateful to them - and Carl's predecessor Malcolm Kemp - as their knowledgeable support has provided me with the backing, relaxed environment and confidence to commentate worldwide on the great passion of my life. That is especially true of the Challenge Cup which, despite my escapades when broadcasting on international matches, Lions tours or World Cups, has given me my most magical moments and a few embarrassments too.

The steady ticking of a large carriage clock sitting on top of a cabinet in the living room of our small council house in St Helens was probably the first association I had with the Challenge Cup. For every time I glanced at the clock before leaving to catch my bus for school I could not fail to notice the small, engraved silver plate attached to it indicating that the time piece had been presented to my dad in recognition of his man of the match performance as captain of his local works amateur team, United Glass Bottles, against the then mighty Hunslet in the first round of the competition in 1938. And it was with my dad and all his mates that, as a lad, I made my first trip 'Up for' t Cup' in 1953 to watch Saints play Huddersfield at Wembley Stadium via the works outing. We set off on a train leaving St Helens at midnight and, after a seven-hour journey, arrived at Euston Station and the prospect of a further three-hour trek around the capital to see the sights of the city. The train should have left on the return leg at 10.00pm but was delayed for two hours owing to the amount of bottled beer the men had to load into the Guard's van. Little did I realise that, when twelve months earlier I had experienced my first introduction to the Challenge Cup and television, I would later enjoy such a lengthy relationship with the game's most prestigious tournament and the then fledgling broadcasting medium.

Again, it was my dad and his enthusiasm for rugby league which were responsible for me standing on a chair alongside him in the basement of our local Co-operative store in the centre of town, in the company of at least another hundred potential customers, all of whom were watching the first ever BBC TV broadcast of a Challenge Cup Final into northern homes. On that eventful April Saturday afternoon in 1952, the electrical department of the St Helens Co-op was packed with men and young lads; not a single woman was to be seen anywhere on the basement floor of the building. No one was inspecting the newly introduced refrigerators or any other of the shiny electrical appliances on sale, all eyes were fixed on the small brown television set perched on top of a large stand and all were straining to see the action being shown on an even tinier nine inch screen. Cheers and roars greeted the fine play and goals of Workington Town's skipper Gus Risman or a try at the corner from Featherstone Rovers' winger Eric Batten after first sidestepping three defenders on his way to the line. But, with television still in its infancy, such acclamation was, every eight minutes, accompanied by even louder groans from the viewers whenever the number four bus passed on its way to Parr and caused such interference to the primitive set that the picture became a mass of white and black dots and flashes. And, of course, it usually occurred at the most exciting times in the match.

Never could I ever have imagined that I and one of the two gentlemen to whom I was listening would, except for a gap between 1953 and 1957 when the Rugby Football League refused to allow the match to be shown on television, be behind the microphone for the Challenge Cup final for over fifty years. Alan Dixon, a regular broadcaster on rugby league on BBC radio's northern programme was the lead commentator that day for the only time in his career and the man sitting alongside him and adapting to the role of an early summariser, Eddie Waring, went on to describe the next twenty-four Wembley occasions. It was my good fortune to be allowed to commentate on the next twenty-seven, from 1982 to 2008, until my colleague Dave Woods took his seat in the TV gantry at Wembley Stadium to animate the Warrington Wolves versus Huddersfield Giants clash. Hopefully that will see him begin an equally as lengthy stint to that of Eddie and myself. At least, thankfully for Dave, on his first occasion, he didn't suffer a similar dramatic interruption to that which certainly unsettled me back in 1982 when I first experienced the demands of speaking to millions of viewers from the national stadium.

Throughout the whole of my playing and commentating career, I have never been troubled with nerves before any match or commentary. In fact, the only time I have ever been so afflicted was when I joined the fans on the terraces to watch my son Gary play in the under-11s curtain-raiser before the Wakefield Trinity and Widnes showdown at the then Twin Towers in 1979. I paced up and down the Wembley terraces anonymously and agonisingly until the St Helens schools team had triumphed by fifteen points to five over a lively Wakefield outfit. However, having prepared myself for my first broadcast and been encouraged by Cliff

Morgan, the BBC's Head of Sport, who so generously left his seat at the pre-match dining table to walk around the stadium and climb to the gantry to offer me his best wishes, I was ready for kick-off. All was going well until, fifteen minutes into the match between Hull and Widnes, I was informed through my earphones by our producer Keith Phillips that British forces had invaded the Falkland Islands just hours before and that, when he instructed me, I was to hand over to Jan Leeming in the BBC Studios who was to deliver a newsflash announcing the dramatic events. I couldn't concentrate on the action below me, my mind occupied with the gravity of the situation and thinking of the words I would use to announce a departure from the match coverage to enable the viewers to hear what would be an historic incident in British history. For the following five or six minutes I wasn't bothered whether Hull's Steve Norton delivered a defence splitting pass to his skipper David Topliss or Widnes full-back Mick Burke had pulled off a superb tackle in midfield. All I could think about was making sure I didn't 'cock up' such an important handover to Jan before millions of viewers at such a dramatic moment on BBC Television. That I succeeded, however, added to my enjoyment of the match, a fourteen-all draw - the only stalemate I ever had the pleasure of being at the microphone for.

There were many occasions during those commentaries when my voice moved up an octave or two and the viewer at home had to turn down the volume on their set. Few tries were more clinically constructed and yet simple in their execution than the wonderful effort from Hull skipper Topliss in the final minute before half-time of the replay of my first Final at Elland Road, Leeds. Having received a long pass from the base of a scrum from his half-back partner Ken Dean, 'Toppo' worked a superb run-around move with his

Kiwi centre, James Leuluai and continued to race through a gap to the line for a try, scored seemingly in the blinking of an eye and without any Widnes defender touching him. There were touchdowns galore to satisfy even the most grudging of rugby league supporters in the 1985 battle between Hull and Wigan, a classic which ended 28-24 in Wigan's favour and which caused my summariser Alex Murphy to insist: 'If we had a try of the season we'd have them all in this game.' Some of the best efforts I have ever described came in that wonderful contest, not least the individual score from James Leuluai who, on receiving the ball from Fred Ah Kuoi's intelligent pass, delivered a breathtaking short, neat sidestep before racing over sixty metres to the try line. That was matched by the four-pointer from Wigan's Aussie stand-off Brett Kenny, who had the crowd and myself standing on our feet as he displayed his blistering speed from halfway before finally racing with ease around Hull full-back Gary Kemble to cross out wide.

Martin Offiah's ninety metre try for Wigan against Leeds in 1994 and his toying with the helpless Loiners' full-back Alan Tait, as he turned him both inside and out with his subtle changes of pace and swerves, must be considered one of the greatest tries ever scored at Wembley, but a match clinching try by diminutive Castleford winger Jamie Sandy against the favourites Hull KR eight years earlier stays firm in my memory. The tiny flyer broke free about forty metres from Rovers' try line and, hotly pursued by at least four defenders, scampered as fast and as bravely as his small legs would carry him. The BBC's overhead camera caught his flight from his pursuers perfectly before he dived over the line with a couple gallantly clinging onto him. Great tries and great tackles too, never better than when, with St Helens trailing by one point to Halifax in a 19-18 thriller in 1987, Fax loose forward John Pendlebury made a desperate tackle in the seventy-second minute on Saints' dashing centre Mark Elia as he was diving over and about to place the ball down for the seeming clincher. A last gasp strike by Pendlebury at Elia's ball carrying arm and the ball was lost, as was the game for my old club.

Wigan's record run of eight successive victories in a Challenge Cup final between 1988 and 1995 will never be forgotten but it will forever be their shock defeat by seventeen points to eight in 1998 to Sheffield Eagles which I will always recall, not for the quality of the play from both sides but for the sheer intensity of the drama which built up as the final minutes ticked away and the sense of disbelief I felt on the gantry when the mighty Wigan, the thirteen-to-one on favourites to lift the trophy, were beaten. Until the last minute, I kept looking incredulously at my co-commentator Joe Lydon who stared back as if in a state of shock. In those final dramatic minutes, I still expected Wigan's Jason Robinson, Kris Radlinski or Dean Bell to conjure up a try or two to snatch victory but it was amazingly not to happen as the Eagles skipper and their Lance Todd Trophy winner for man of the match, Mark Aston, held firm and created the biggest upset in the history of BBC TV's coverage of the tournament. A record was set in another all-action thirteen-try thriller between St Helens and Bradford Bulls in 1996, a game fondly remembered by myself but maybe not so by those Bulls viewers who gripped their armchairs with ever whiter knuckles as the horror of their team's defeat, after holding a 26-12 lead approaching the hour, unfolded. A first ever hat-trick of tries at Wembley by the Bulls half-back maestro Robbie Paul proved of little avail as his nemesis Bobbie Goulding hit back in the final quarter with a series of towering kicks which taunted and teased Bradford's unfortunate custodian Nathan Graham and resulted in three tries and an unexpected 40-32 win for the Saints. And although it was not among the best of matches to grace the Wembley turf, I was especially pleased to hold the microphone throughout one of the most significant contests to be held at the famous stadium - the cross channel clash between St Helens and Catalans Dragons from Perpignan in 2007. How delighted and proud would those men have been who authorised the brave decision to take the Challenge Cup final to London and Wembley Stadium in 1929, to see a French team competing in the decider of the code's major knockout tournament.

Many and varied have been the summarisers or co-commentators who have climbed the steps to the television position with me but the former Wigan coach John Monie, a valued companion in the commentary box on other occasions, was never able to offer his astute and knowledgeable insight to the millions of Challenge Cup Final viewers. I know, however, that he wasn't too concerned, for his absence was invariably caused by regularly sitting on the coach's bench and guiding Wigan to yet another of those record breaking eight successive victories. Former rugby league players and coaches Keith Fielding, Allan Agar, Maurice Bamford, Peter Fox, Steve Simms, Terry Flanagan, Joe Lydon and ex-London Broncos' Aussie boss Ross Strudwick - the only man I know who, having forgotten to bring his tickets and passes to the 1992 final, gained entrance to Wembley Stadium and access to the TV gantry without any documents - all lent their expertise to the broadcasts. But by far the most regular visitors to the box were my good mates and regular verbal sparring partners Alex Murphy and Jonathan Davies, two of the finest ever half-backs but also a pair of the most enjoyable characters to work with on any live event. Rugby league half-backs have a tendency to chatter and chirp throughout the eighty minutes of a match, cajoling or cursing the forwards lumbering in front of them but always having the sense of humour to raise a smile with a caustic comment to the opposition. As my grandmother used to say of a lady in our avenue, 'She could fall out with herself in a back entry,' so I have always found can scrum-halves, but I love them for it. Both Alex and Jonathan have two of the shrewdest rugby brains, can analyse an incident almost without thinking and are not afraid to offer an honest opinion no matter how controversial. Their sense of humour, arguments with me and the often outrageous banter between us have, I believe, brightened many a dull match and possibly eased many casual viewers into a liking for and following of the game. Above all, the duo have the ability to pass comment on the replay of a try with the brevity and clarity needed in the few seconds available to them, unlike one famous former player who brought a writing pad full of notes on everyone in both teams to assist him with his comments in the event of a try. Unfortunately, by the time my summariser had opened his pad at the relevant page and digested the facts on the try scorer, the television replay had finished and the goal kicker was attempting the conversion.

In more recent years, as viewers have become more interested in and aware of the tactical aspects of rugby league, so the opinions of current leading coaches and players like Robbie Paul, John Kear, Ian Millward, Justin Morgan, Brian Noble and company have been well received by the viewers. Strong opinion on a player or an incident is always welcome even though outspoken views might be divisive in an audience. All have served and continue to serve BBC TV and rugby league well but some, like Joe Lydon, have come to my rescue magnificently in times of stress and strain during a match commentary at Wembley. Reflecting back on that never to be forgotten 1998 Final between giantkillers Sheffield Eagles and the supposedly untouchable Wigan, the tension as we approached the closing stages of a pulsating game was gripping the viewers but few will have been under as much pressure - literally - as I was. Having been introduced for the first time to the delights of bottled sparkling water at lunch prior to the game, I took three bottles of the supposed elixir of life up to the microphone for use during the couple of hours pre-match work and for during the actual game itself; completely forgetting that there was no toilet sited anywhere near our commentary position in the old Wembley Stadium. After my consumption of almost four bottles, I was desperate to relieve myself with half an hour to go and the presentations still to come. Desperate situations called for extreme measures. A constant movement of my eyes during my commentary alerted Joe to the fact that I wanted him to get hold of an old red, tin fire bucket, a silent request which he duly carried out and promptly held the bucket where, while I in full flow at the microphone I could be in full flow elsewhere. The flow elsewhere was too strong and fast, causing Malcolm Kemp our match producer to bark into my headphones: 'Ray, I can hear water. Have we got a leak somewhere? I'm sending an electrician up there, can't be too careful.' Neither Malcolm nor the electrician ever found the source of the leak.

No commentator can afford to assume that matters will all run smoothly on Cup Final day and I would advise my colleague Dave Woods and his co-commentators to arrive at the stadium in good time and to make their way to the commentary box with at least an hour or two to spare before donning the headphones and grasping the microphone. Or risk the stress and frantic thoughts that ran through my head when it appeared that, thanks to being trapped twice in lifts, I might not make the kick-off or even Wembley Stadium itself. Many refused to trust themselves in the rickety, antiquated lift which ferried people to the floor on which the gantry stood in the old Wembley Stadium but Joe Gormley, the President of the Mineworkers Union and later Lord Gormley Of Ashton in Makerfield OBE, had no such fears when he asked me to show him around our broadcasting position before the Featherstone Rovers against Hull final in 1983. Insisting that he had been down a mine shaft in far worse lifts than the one into which we stepped, he duly pressed the button to start the contraption and we rattled and clanked upwards for about twenty seconds before coming to a juddering, screeching halt. For forty minutes, until we were eventually hauled up silently to our destination, Joe regaled me with stories of worse down the pits while I was tormented with visions of Malcolm Kemp searching frantically for me throughout the endless corridors of the stadium. Worse was to come ahead of my last commentary from the new Wembley in 2008 when, along with some St Helens supporters, I was stuck in the lift of the hotel actually on the site of the Stadium only an hour before I was due to voice over a short tribute to the late Don Fox, who sadly but sensationally missed what would have been a match winning goal from in front of the goalposts against Leeds in the 1968 'watersplash' final. As a friend of mine, and in the knowledge that all his family would no doubt be watching the tribute to him, I was in a panic. Luckily, after twenty minutes, the lift was raised slowly to the next floor and the doors were burst open by a couple of firemen. Without pausing to say, 'Thank you,' I dashed down the fire escape to the ground floor and raced to the ground to start work, but not before a pause for breath and a welcome cup of tea.

The future relationship between sport, especially rugby league, television and even radio is difficult to predict. Here, the BBC and Sky TV dominate the scene yet the advances in technology with the internet, mobile phones and other such gadgetry is so rapid that one wonders how millions worldwide will, in fifty years time, be following the action in the Challenge Cup. I hope that if commentators, summarisers, co-commentators, studio guests, touchline news gatherers - call them what you will - are still finding work and the main broadcasters are continuing to promote our great game, that the Beeb will use only two commentators on a live broadcast and not three as they once did and that Sky - one day - will allow their main two, Mike Stephenson and Eddie Hemmings, to command the air during the actual match commentary itself and not be interrupted by at least another four or five 'experts'. Too many with microphones make for speaking for speaking's sake and the natural passion and character of the men behind them, which can bind them to the viewer, is often lost. A television picture can tell its own story, a voice is only needed to embellish it, highlight the background to any action and assess its significance to the match. The current close association between rugby league and its broadcast partners is a far cry from the days when, in 1969, a large number of clubs met at Oldham for a meeting to seek ways of ending a live TV contract immediately, such was their fear of the reduction in gates most clubs were then experiencing. Today, apart from providing its major function of entertainment, television can enhance the profile of rugby league, spread the impact of the code at both amateur and professional levels, help increase attendances at matches and provide the game with a very valuable, almost indispensable, income stream.

16

Size Isn't Everything

'TRYLESS, witless and clueless,' and 'a turgid mess' were but a couple of the scathing headlines which greeted England's rugby union performances during the 2010 Six Nations tournament. 'Wrestling too much a part of the game,' and 'referee's "go slow" rulings spoil the spectacle,' were headlines which similarly greeted the opening matches of the same year's engage Super League season. So, all is apparently not well with both codes of rugby and both in a state of decline as sporting attractions. Well, hardly, if the levels of interest recorded via the media and through the turnstiles are any indication. Both BBC TV and Sky have announced healthy and rising viewing figures for their coverage of both league and union while attendances in the rugby union's Guinness Premiership and the rugby league's premier competition are on the increase. A union club like Leicester Tigers are forced to enlarge and make improvements to their stadium in order to cope with the numbers of fans wanting to support them, while St Helens and Salford City Reds in league are endeavouring to realise their plans for new grounds and have them completed within the next twelve to eighteen months. Profitable World Cups, whether at home or abroad, are on the immediate horizon for both sports and union's Six Nations and league's Four Nations tournaments continue to attract major sponsors and crowds whatever the playing standards of the competing nations.

Where, then, lies the problem for the two sports, if there really is one? Is there a common theme which is responsible for such negative vocabulary and descriptions and, if so, are the causes really so detrimental to one's enjoyment of a modern game of rugby? I have always believed that the primary aim when playing both codes is to run with and pass the ball in an attempt to score tries.

It is a concept shared with the majority of supporters of both codes which is why fans find themselves so vehemently bemoaning the manner in which the ball is recycled into play when a player is tackled and brought to ground. For over a century, both league and union have battled to come to terms with the techniques and rules best employed as to how a tackled player releases the ball, while football has no such problems. Quite simply, the one obvious advantage of football - and I insist there is only one - is that there is effectively no breakdown in play and, unlike rugby, the game is simple to play by virtue of its continuity, hence its universal popularity. With the oval ball, after the player in possession has been legally brought to ground, there are rules demanding where defenders can position themselves, the length of time a player can hold the ball or the tackler can restrain them, leaving plenty for the hapless referee to invigilate.

In union, vast numbers of penalties are incurred by the actions of players arriving at the breakdown of play. Huge forwards drive ever forward monotonously with a 'pick up and go' technique around the ruck area and half-backs often kick aimlessly downfield to gain position and remove the threat of one of many likely penalties being awarded within sight of their goal posts. Crucially too, and to the detriment of quality running and handling - most especially for frustrated backs - there is such little space allowed within the rules between the teams be it at ruck, maul or scrum.

The Rugby Football Union's head of elite referees, Ed Morrison, summed up the situation during the 2010 Six Nations tournament when he said: 'The breakdown is damned hard for referees because there are so many athletic players arriving so quickly, whereas in the past only one or two arrived quickly and the others got there when the ball was gone. Now all twenty-three in the squad have the skill and power to enter that area and contest it, not just the back-row forwards.' What further reinforces his observations is the staggering statistic that the average weight of every back in all of the Six Nations teams was over fourteen stone per man and that the French line-up contained Yannick Jauzion and Aurelien Rougerie at sixteen and a half stone and the massive seventeen stone four pound Mathieu Bastareaud at centre. That further indicates how the lack of space is leading to bigger and more powerful men being used behind the pack to bludgeon their way through rather than use the ball.

As Paddy O'Brien, the International Rugby Union Board's elite referee manager, sensibly insists in support of his colleague Mr Morrison's complaints: 'The game is about space, the law is there to preserve space and we have to do it better.' In both codes of rugby, for over a hundred years, space was also effected by the bigger players tiring as the attritional contests wore on but, sadly that is also not now the case owing to the vast number of substitutes and interchange players available off the bench. A reduction in the number allowed - the Australian Rugby League have reduced theirs in the domestic competition from twelve to eight with huge success - would help create a more open play and allow smaller, lighter backs to display their pace, swerve and sidesteps. The sort of skills that were the staple diets of the likes of former union international stars Jeremy Guscott, Barry John, David Watkins, Phil Bennett, Jonathan Davies, John Horton, Richard Sharpe, Philippe Sella and company. Hopefully then we would see more than the six tries in total being scored by England throughout all of their Six Nations matches, as witnessed in 2010.

Whatever changes to the rules are required by rugby union to restore the domestic game to being primarily a running and handling one with tries at its core, I confess to not having the technical expertise to suggest. But I would insist that, as in rugby league, the belief in pumping iron daily in the gymnasium and the inescapable, modern cult of the 'fitter, faster, stronger' mentality is taking its toll. Rugby union's major problem today in its attempts to clear the immobile morass of humanity which often clutters up its pitches, is the fact that its legislators appear not to recognise the fact that, as the code's players have become large, fast, fit athletes, the size of the pitch has remained virtually the same as it was in 1895. In short, today there are too many powerful professionals on the pitch compared to those fatter and slower amateurs who used to amble around in their specialist positions, which was one of the main attractions to play. The inability to pierce defences regularly now in union has also been made all the harder by the fifteen-a-side code's infatuation with employing former rugby league personalities like Shaun Edwards, Mike Ford, Alan Tait and David Ellis principally to improve their defensive discipline and structure. Their ideas and regimes have proved so effective that again space is at a premium and power, especially in the centres, the overriding tactic. Former Great Britain RL and Munster RU winger and now Sky presenter Brian Carney believes that: 'the use of defence coaches from rugby league has taught union players, who once placed little emphasis on collective defensive techniques and routines, the importance of defending and tackling as a unit. The problem for the game now is that it is so much more easy to defend with fifteen players than thirteen players. The players are just too fit and they are rarely given the chance to tire.'

That strength, fitness, energy and size of union's modern gladiators, especially among its forwards, has also led to problems with the scrummage at the highest levels, so much so that the International Rugby Union Board has recently seen fit to re-assess an area which was rightly once the pride and joy of its devotees. No doubt having tired of watching almost three-quarters of all scrums in the Six Nations Tournament matches collapse or have to be reformed, Paddy O'Brien was moved to say: 'We have to do something about the scrum, it's unacceptable for a scrum to take more than two minutes thirty seconds to be completed.' Mr O'Brien would also do well to listen to BBC commentator and former England RU hooker Brian Moore, constantly but correctly bemoaning the incidence of crooked feeding of the ball at the scrum, a practice which undermines the myths of the significance and superiority of the union scrum as opposed to those formed in league.

It is misleading for both the union media and any of the bigots of rugby league to pillory union backs for their apparent lack of flair and adventure for it is the rules and style of play which is putting a stop to the likes of Ireland's Tommy Bowe and Brian O'Driscoll, Wales' James Hock and Shane Williams and England's Ben Foden from displaying all too rarely their undoubted attacking talents. It is to a somewhat lesser extent happening in certain areas of the game in rugby league, but having only thirteen men per side and an actual stoppage in play every time a player is tackled, does allow for a greater clearance of bodies and less chance of a foul up at the play the ball re-start. Sky TV's rugby union analyst Stuart Barnes is quite right when, following Toulouse RU's narrow Heineken Cup triumph in Paris in 2010 over their fellow countrymen of Biarritz, he criticised the winners for not capitalising on their total domination of the match in the scrums. He correctly insisted in his newspaper column: 'The sport has scope to acclaim the power of the scrum, but if it is to earn the exposure of the non-rugby world, it has to have more of a capacity to dream than we saw from yesterday's winners. The charge sheet worsens when one looks at the brimful of brilliance in the Toulouse backline. Nobody was screaming for them to throw the ball willy-nilly from one side of the pitch to the other, but a bolder policy with so much scrum ball on the front foot, would not only have given the neutral entertainment, but, more importantly, Toulouse would have scored the tries to provide breathing space.' Unfortunately, if the union code continues to ally fifteen fitter, faster, bigger and stronger players with well coached league defensive patterns on a standard-sized pitch, tries from any back division will be at a premium.

Thankfully there is no free for all in rugby league at the breakdown and only four players, at all times under the close eye of the referee, involved in the recycling of the ball at the ensuing play. All other protagonists are at least - in theory - ten metres apart and there is a stoppage while the ball is in the act of being brought back into jurisdiction. It is, however, the length of that stoppage and the time taken before the tackled player is allowed to play the ball, not the seemingly chaotic collisions and pile-ups which blight the union code, which present problems for those who wish to achieve a seamless continuity in rugby league. Wrestling techniques, turning the tackled player on his back, lying on the ball carrier and other assorted practices have, in recent seasons, slowed down the playing of the ball and, as in union, allowed defences to realign and gain the upper hand. Rugby league is seen at its best when good teams are allowed to play the ball at speed and the acting half-back is able to gain momentum with the set of six tackles available to him. It is necessary, therefore, that strict and uniform policing by the referees is the order of the day and that infringements are dealt with quickly and regularly. There is little wrong with wrestling techniques being introduced to the game if they are applied within the rules. I should say re-introduced, for wrestling techniques both in the making and evading of a tackle, were common in the Fifties and Sixties with players like St Helens second-rower Bill Bretherton and others regularly receiving instruction in local wrestling gyms. The problems currently affecting the game in that area have been addressed in Australia by the use of two referees, the sole duty of one being to police the play the ball. No longer can Melbourne Storm do at home what they were allowed to when stifling Leeds Rhinos in the 2010 Carnegie World Club Challenge, by suffocating their speed after a tackle. Conversely, we appear to be going down that road here and there is a very real danger of creating the same sport played under two different sets of rules in the respective hemispheres.

The scrum in rugby league, owing to the fact that the six-man pack, unlike in union, lacks the two stabilisers (flankers) on the sides, has long been a pale shadow of that formed in the union code. More so since the emasculating of the league scrum by the introduction of rules allowing the feeding of the ball and the current practice of there being little or no pushing from any of the supposedly competing forwards. The scrum in league is today seen by many as merely another means of restarting play after an infringement and the hooker, once primarily a ball winner, is now the ball distributor in midfield as he links up at acting half with his half-back colleagues. There are even those, like Leigh Centurions' leading Aussie coach Ian Millward, who perceive the scrum as an irrelevance in the modern game and can see no basis or purpose for it in a coach's tactics. He insists: 'Scrums have virtually nothing to offer the modern game of rugby league. All they do is break the flow and momentum of matches and waste vital minutes of the game. We want our product to be as fast as possible, but all scrums are is a chance for players to catch their breath or settle back down once they have made an error. Rugby league scrums are just a waste of time. There is no skill or technique in a scrum any more. What I'm suggesting is get rid of the scrums altogether.'

Shame on you, Ian! If you use a scrum to allow your players to catch their breath and cannot see any possibilities of attack from the set piece situation, then you hardly warrant the high estimation I have for your coaching skills. Even though the outcome of a league scrum is invariably a foregone conclusion, I have seen many tries scored and attacking ploys advanced by clever switching of play and innovative moves behind it. Some of the most exciting touchdowns scored are created by the coach who dares to allow a player to kick the ball on the first tackle when the opposition back line is lying up and flat and the full-back is at a disadvantage. Are run-around moves at half-back or in the centre a thing of the past? Certainly not if adventure is coached in a side. What about play between a ball handling loose forward and the halves? Especially if, as should be the case, the rule policing the emergence of the ball at the back of the scrum insisted that the defending loose forward could only break once it had passed into the hands of the opposing scrum half. The pack still gathers the forwards together as a unit and allows for greater space in which creative backs can launch an attack rather than merely soak up the first tackle of a set and seeing the defensive line continually stretched across the field. The scrum still offers a variety of restart and movement which is a relief from the all too flat and predictable play offered up by many coaches who would have us all playing touch rugby if we left rule making to them.

The current obsession with flat, one-dimensional rugby league, though still exciting, entertaining and full of passion and skill, has changed the balance and make up of teams physically. As we have seen in union, size is often the determining factor when choosing a three-quarter line and we now even see players of the bulk and height of St Helens' Leon Pryce and Wakefield Trinity Wildcats' Paul Cooke starring at stand-off. How many players like Huddersfield Giants' Lee Gilmour, St Helens' Chris Flannery or Dane Carlaw of Catalans Dragons are now valued for being able to play in both the second row and centre equally effectively? Why is it that the interchange bench of any Super League team invariably contains the names of four forwards or, on all too rare occasions, just one back? It is because the game is veering far too much towards the physical aspects of the play and losing the precocious skills of smaller men who are or were far more evasive and blessed with the balance and pace to run around rather than through their opponents. I well remember during my playing days at St Helens centres of the calibre of Ken Large, Brian McGinn and Ken Williams, who were not the biggest of men but were allowed to give full rein to their talents thanks to the rules then in operation. And what a delight to see international centres of a similar build like Wakefield Trinity's Ian Brooke, Hull KR's Alan Burwell and Swinton's Alan Buckley in full flight with the ball. Today would they be demoted to being the lonely back sitting alongside three forwards on the interchange bench? I hope not but the demands of the modern game in both codes would seem to have the smaller, agile, thrilling backs missing out in selection.

As stronger, fitter and faster full-time forwards cover so many more metres across the pitch as their part-time counterparts in the packs of yesteryear, what too of the wingers in rugby league? Are the rules and tactics employed still allowing them to fulfil the role so loved by fans of eras past? Hardly. For all the abilities and finishing prowess of leading practitioners - in 2010 Wigan's Pat Richards and Darrell Goulding, Huddersfield's David Hodgson, St Helens pair Ade Gardner and Francis Meli, Leeds Rhinos duo Scott Donald and Ryan Hall, Hull KR's Peter Fox and Warrington Wolves' emerging wing flyer, Chris Riley, scoring tries via a sidestep, swerve or blistering pace on the outside of a defender down the touchline, the staple diet of a traditional flank flyer - would seem to be just one requirement today. I was intrigued by comments made by Leeds' shrewd coach, Kiwi Brian McClennan, regarding the signing of a new four-year deal by his club's outstanding international winger, Hall. I don't dispute what Brian said but his reflections amply indicate the changes of the last decade or two and alterations to the rules that have altered the way wingers now play. 'You can't rate him on how many tries he scores. Obviously we want him to continue to be a good finisher but there is more to it. He should be judged on his kick returns, the way he positions himself, the way he recovers the ball and the decisions he makes defensively.' Sensible comment from a coach grappling with the demands of the modern game and its requirements but how, I wonder, would our coaches react if confronted with the likes of the greatest of wingers of days of yore such as Len Killeen, Mick Sullivan, Ike Southward, Martin Offiah and their ilk? Would Brian Bevan, the scorer of 796 tries and whose idea of defence was, 'take him, he's yours' be cast aside as inadequate? Would legendary Welsh winger Billy Boston be judged on his 'kick returns'? Which style of wing play do the fans really want to see? The prolific try scoring and daring touchline dashes of St Helens' famous Springbok Tom van Vollenhoven or the added all round action of a Pat Richards? Two very fine wingers playing to and taking advantage of the rules current in their eras but which is the more attractive to watch even for the young generation? I think I know but let not misty eyes and rose tinted spectacles confuse my judgement.

Whatever the era and no matter what the rules, one factor remains constant, great rugby league players will always be exactly that. Rugby League Hall of Fame legends Jim Sullivan, Gus Risman, Alex Murphy, Harold Wagstaff, Albert Rosenfeld, Billy Batten and the rest would still be the greatest of stars if playing today. And I am sure that seasoned Test players of recent decades like Jamie Peacock, Adrian Morley, Keith Senior, Keiron Cunningham and Sean Long would still catch the eye if playing in teams of forty, fifty or sixty years ago. Class is timeless and great players would adjust. But no matter what one thinks of the current playing styles of both codes with the seemingly endless, aimless kicking, the lack of incisive running behind the scrum in union and the often over regimentation and dominant physical confrontation of league, both codes appear to be in good health and with an ever increasing audience watching both live and on TV, at elite club and international levels. In the current harsh economic times, that says much for the loyalty and faith of the traditional supporters of the respective codes and the attractiveness of the spectacle - or naivety - of new ones.

Admittedly, in both codes at the semi-professional levels once major union clubs like Coventry, London Welsh, Birmingham/Solihull, Manchester, and Waterloo and counterparts such as Keighley Cougars, Doncaster, Workington Town, Gateshead Thunder and others, have found it difficult to generate the income needed to sustain their ambitions. Thanks to a saturation of top, live sport on TV and an ever increasing mentality in Britain of only supporting winners, it is becoming harder for both codes of rugby to attract crowds to many matches below the top tier of competition. The realisation by the marketeers and media corps of both games that once normal, everyday matches must now be sold as events to attract and nurture new supporters and to retain and stop the faithful from being distracted or tempted by other offerings, has produced good results and established greater prominence among the general public and attendant media.

The RFU has a strong hold in London and is boosted by the presence of many wealthy and famous clubs in the capital like Saracens, Harlequins and London Irish. It has immediate access to state of the art stadiums at Twickenham and Wembley, so it is little wonder that their staging of showcases to boost crowds and awareness of the very game itself has been a huge success. The atmosphere and attractions surrounding matches staged by London Irish and Wasps, for example, to celebrate St Patrick's Day and St George's Day have generated huge numbers while the decision of Harlequins' management to switch their Boxing Day Guinness Premiership fixture from their Stoop Memorial ground to the nearby, palatial Twickenham Stadium generated a record seventy thousand gate instead of their normal ten thousand-plus attendance. Saracens welcomed the South African touring side to a friendly contest at Wembley and were rewarded with a turn up approaching the fifty thousand mark. Surrounded by good old fashioned razzmatazz, cheaper ticketing and inventive sponsorship and hospitality packages, the union code has proved that such specially marketed features do arouse a greater interest in the sport by many who only occasionally visit or want to experience a game having looked on from the outside, initially via TV. Rugby league, despite the minority of vociferous supporters who still believe that any match staged ten miles south of Brighouse is heresy but who, thankfully, are now being ignored by the code's more enlightened governing body, is also at the forefront in raising the awareness of its appeal locally and nationally. More adventurous Super League clubs, like Wigan Warriors, are building a theme into and around a particular match and setting a target attendance figure for it. Clubs are staging special 'family days', featuring all inclusive cheaper ticketing and extensive entertainment surrounding the actual eighty minutes of action, both inside and outside the stadium. The introduction of the 'Millennium Magic' and, subsequently, 'Murrayfield Magic' weekends in Cardiff and Edinburgh, when a complete programme of seven top flight matches are staged at the famous rugby union grounds over a bank holiday weekend - and where a carnival atmosphere reigns in the cities for forty-eight hours or more - have proved a big attraction to fans old and new. The World Club Challenge between the Southern and Northern Hemisphere champion teams, despite the problems of travel for the 'away' club, has proved a very popular fixture when staged at football grounds like Elland Road, Leeds or the Reebok Stadium, Bolton. The 'Day at the Seaside' at Blackpool for the playing of the Northern Rail Cup Final is now an eagerly awaited event in the calendar for fans of lower division clubs.

In both forms of rugby, the governing bodies must take heed of the growing attractions of other sports and realise they are part of the entertainment industry. The match must be celebrated as an occasion and spectators drawn to it by the comforts of the stadium itself, warmth of the welcome and accompanying added value as well as the very quality of the fare on offer on the pitch. Rugby league, by virtue of the greater space and freedom and emphasis on a talented individual's creativity and flair, can still provide exciting and tense action in both attack and defence and, importantly, usually spectacular tries. Rugby union has surely exceeded all expectations when the game turned professional, internationals maintaining their prominence and the spillover being seen at its Guinness Premiership and Heineken Cup matches. And yet, although the fifteen-a-side game still successfully trades heavily on its social cachet, for how much longer can it continue to attract the masses to watch an ever decreasing level of entertainment on the pitch? An intriguing situation summed up admirably by *The Times'* award winning columnist Simon Barnes and succinctly highlighted by his namesake, the former England RU half-back and Sky's union commentator Stuart Barnes.

According to Simon: 'The Twickenham faithful are now faithless. They turned up all right, they turned up in their usual thousands, past lines of touts trying to buy rather than sell. There's no shortage of bodies in the stadium. People are turning up to Twickenham for the craic, for a day out, for the sightseeing, for a day of ritual licence and booze. They are not turning up because they believe in the England team. They have a good old drink and grouse about how things used to be.'

Stuart similarly, and incredulously, queries the increasing

interest surrounding rugby union's major games. 'There seems to be some sort of mysterious law of inverse logic: the worse the rugby, the bigger the crowds. The thrill of the Heineken Cup has only highlighted the glaring discrepancies in the quality of the domestic game but still the crowds flock to matches. The thought of that endless wait to escape Twickenham's Siberian clutches after the final whistle has had no impact on ticket sales. People want their club rugby whatever the quality. How can this fanaticism be explained?'

Whatever the answer to his apposite question - one which I am sure cannot be answered on the time honoured postcard - I can only acknowledge the reality of it and the truth of these observations. I have always enjoyed playing, coaching and watching rugby union, have a vast number of friends within the game and am proud to have been the president of my former club, Liverpool St Helens, for the past ten years. However, I now much prefer to watch the sport at local level, where the ball is still passed around and tries are scored by willing amateurs than suffer the often dreary stodge served up at international and senior level at Twickenham and elsewhere. Despite the arguments surrounding the attractions or otherwise of rugby union, I still retain my interest and support and always will, but it is rugby league, one of the great passions of my life, which never fails to excite me and which can offer the finest of entertainment and enjoyment to those who are willing to try it - as a player or spectator. Rugby union, because of how it stole the limelight via the establishment, continues to hold its position as the dominant rugby code worldwide but rugby league, thanks to its more simplistic format, its more open and individual style of play and damned hard work from bands of willing volunteers and a host of energetic development officers is prospering as never before and is, at last, reaching the places once considered out of bounds.

When I journeyed to a school in the midlands back in the early Eighties at the request of league pioneer and inspiration behind the Birmingham Bulldogs club John Simkin to talk to youngsters about the prospects of playing rugby league, I never dreamed that the city of Birmingham would, a quarter of a century later, be hosting a Champion Schools tournament featuring five age groups from eleven to sixteen years old. Nor did I ever envisage that in 2010 a schools under-16s Championship would be held between youngsters representing Saudi Arabia, Palestine and Lebanon while, almost at the same time, universities and colleges in the West Indies would be competing for the Jamaican RL Association's annual trophy. The barriers are down, rugby's apartheid is well and truly over and the thirteen-a-side code has expanded both nationwide and worldwide more in the past ten years than in the previous hundred.

At home, while the British Amateur Rugby League Association continues to underpin the amateur section of the code in the heartlands and helps expansion abroad with its many tours to developing countries, the Co-operative RL Conference divisions, played in the summer months, currently features a record number of more than a hundred teams in a variety of national and local leagues from places as widespread as Bristol, Gloucester, Jarrow, Sunderland, Coventry, North Devon, Southampton, Nottingham, St Albans, Hainault, St Ives, Norwich and Bedford. Though the aim of such expansion throughout England is purely for participation, the Harlequins club has already signed the likes of England international Louie McCarthy-Scarsbrook from Greenwich Admirals, Ben Bolger from St Albans Centurions and also Tony Clubb and Jamie O'Callaghan from the southern leagues. Darrell Griffin, once a winger with Oxford Cavaliers, is now a regular in the pack of the

Huddersfield Giants. In Wales, twelve clubs compete in two leagues and talented amateur players from them are graduating to the professional ranks in the Principality at Neath with South Wales Scorpions and Wrexham for the Crusaders in the Championship and Super League respectively. In Scotland, nine clubs from Edinburgh, Fife, Falkirk and elsewhere are prospering while such is the enthusiasm for rugby league at club and college levels in Ireland that, for the first time, the Ireland Students squad selected for the Students UK Championships in April 2010 were all home grown talent from the Emerald Isle. Rugby league is now a major sport played throughout all universities and colleges in Britain and, as in union, the unique significance of the Oxford against Cambridge encounter is recognised in the annual RL Varsity match between them which superbly presented live on Sky TV. The success of French club Catalans Dragons in the elite has inspired six universities from Perpignan, Girona and Barcelona to compete in a Catalan Universities Championships. The Royal Navy, Army and Royal Air Force enter teams in the early rounds of the prestigious Challenge Cup and an RL Sevens Tag Festival has been daringly held in the war zone of Helmand, Afghanistan for league enthusiasts serving in the British army, South African units and US Marines.

Though rugby league as a sport can never achieve the universality of football or perhaps be played in the number of countries that rugby union has penetrated over the past hundred-plus years, the game's credibility and financial welfare will be more secure for the extensive expansion which has been made in the past couple of decades worldwide, at both professional and amateur levels. That countries like the Czech Republic, Germany, Italy, Russia, Serbia, Ukraine, Latvia, Estonia, Lebanon and elsewhere in

Europe are playing it internationally and fostering their own domestic leagues is a far cry from the days when, in the early Sixties, a ten team league in the then Yugoslavia was aborted and the participants switched to rugby union because the Rugby Football League and its blinkered clubs would not provide the teams with jerseys, at a time when such clothing was extremely expensive in communist countries. The provision of kit by the more far-sighted French rugby union meant that the thirteen-a-side code's days were numbered. An enlightened attitude today has, however, enabled the Rugby League International Federation to expand the proposed 2013 World Cup to fourteen teams from the ten who took part in the tournament in Australia in 2008. Such is the increased participation in the sport around the world that twelve nations will automatically be entered and two more will emerge from qualifying tournaments in the northern and southern hemispheres. Rugby league is at last moving forward rapidly on both the domestic and international fronts by virtue of its own efforts. No longer are there bans in place or social exclusion, nor does a player's workplace halt his progress as a professional. The complete and genuinely free gangway between the two codes, though never truly free until the advent of professionalism in union, is offering different horizons to league players and enabling the sport to enhance its reputation on and off the pitch.

Until that point, despite union having the greater profile, league raided it for some of its ultimately finest exponents, as many of the try, goal and points scoring records of clubs show; Dewsbury (Dai Thomas), Halifax (Tysul Griffiths, Ron James, Johnny Freeman), Huddersfield (Ben Gronow), Hull (Clive Sullivan), Leeds (Lewis Jones), St Helens (Kel Coslett, Tom van Vollenhoven), Salford (Gus Risman, David Watkins, Maurice Richards), Widnes (Jonathan Davies,

Martin Offiah, Mick Burke), Wigan (Jim Sullivan, Johnny Ring, Billy Boston), Workington (Lyn Hopkins, Iain MacCorquodale) for example. The large number of cross-code signings in the past from union to league by outstanding, experienced and renowned players has of course, in recent times, virtually dried up thanks to the large salaries now being paid to the fifteen-a-side stars. The switch from the Ospreys RU club to Crusaders RL early in 2010 by Wales' most capped international player Gareth Thomas is, however, an interesting move; one which shows that there is still the temptation among the leading players to test themselves in the rival code and which is proving to be a pointer for other younger union players to follow. Many young lads, no longer facing bans or defamation from the hypocritical, are now eager to sample what rugby league has to offer and South Wales Scorpions are attracting interest from those who see their future in the game and, possibly, later with Super League outfit Crusaders in Wrexham. Similar numbers of adolescents of a union background are now also finding their way to the Harlequins RL club in an effort to make their way in the alternative code. It is no longer a big pay packet which is attracting them but the fact that they feel their talents, differing physiques and instinctive flair might be more suited to advancement in league rather than in union.

Conversely, the considerable movement of traffic from league to union in the past decade has produced little stunning success apart from Wigan's Jason Robinson, for both player and code alike. Andy Farrell, Lesley Vainikolo, Iestyn Harris and Henry Paul were among those who had the honour of becoming dual internationals following their switch of codes but Farrell, one of the true greats of rugby league was troubled with injuries after a lifetime in league and was, in fact, playing at prop forward in his natural game when he switched to the centre role for England RU. That says something about his abilities but it also tells more about the style of play in modern rugby union. Big Lesley was wracked with knee problems before leaving for pastures new with Gloucester RU club and, although still a fearsome threat on the wing, has never reached the heights in union he did in league. And, quite frankly, the Wales and England RU coaching teams didn't have a clue what to do with and where to play Iestyn and Henry, two of the most gifted individuals in league. It would appear union is at last learning that, on account of the multiplicity of unit skills within the game, it is a much more difficult game than rugby league for any convert to master. It is no coincidence that the snaring of youngsters Chris Ashton and Stephen Myler by Northampton and Gloucester RU has been more of a success recently, because both have been given time to learn and adapt to their new sport out of the initial glare of the spotlight.

Whatever the misgivings concerning the impact made on the union code by league converts, their presence, personality and attitude in the fifteen-a-side environment has helped to foster a much better image and understanding of the game of rugby league than was once present within many union circles, where a misguided and laughable social snobbery once existed against those whose palms were crossed with silver. Albeit legally!

It is heartening that more like me, though having a passion for one code of rugby, can enjoy and even take part in and contribute to the welfare of the other. And yet I would add that my definition and application of the word 'rugby', which has given me so much enjoyment and, at times, heartache, appears to be somewhat different to that currently being aired by the rugby union code's governing bodies and even by certain misguided souls within the media.

17

Looking Forward

IF any reader of this book has walked into a Marks and Spencer's store during the past twelve months he or she might well have glanced through the contents of a colourful, glossy paperback book on sale in the shop and seemingly produced by the famous retailer, boldly entitled *Rugby*. If our potential customer was a rugby league supporter they might well have been mystified and considered calling Trades Descriptions for, after carefully considering every page and photograph, they would have found no mention of the thirteen-a-side code. Readers of their daily newspaper, too, might well have been confused when, on turning to its sports pages, they were confronted with a dramatic introduction to a sensational article declaring: 'These are troubling times for rugby. The image of the game has been besmirched like never before.' Those of us who pride ourselves in keeping abreast of all happenings in rugby league might well have been concerned at the damage done to our game but, after reading of the 'bloodgate' scandal - when Harlequins RU winger Tom Williams was found guilty of misuse of the blood bin regulations by faking an injury - we were all, no doubt, relieved to learn that the 'troubling times' made no reference to our preferred version of the sport. League devotees were, presumably, full of eager anticipation when they were informed that, in response to an application to participate, the game was set to take its place in the Olympic Games. Speculative comment in the written media warned: 'Rugby is not there yet -confirmation must wait until October - but the battle that has been waged for the past twenty years has nearly been won.' The hurrahs must have rung loud and clear too when they were later confronted with headlines announcing: 'Rugby Sevens in Olympic Games.' But, yet again, disappointment when it was noted that the sevens game to be played was of the union variety. Why such confusion over the naming of sports which demand running and passing with an oval shaped ball? To which does Rugby World Cup refer? On which game does the rugby correspondent of a newspaper or a radio station report?

At the turn of the twentieth century in England, when rugby union players in the south considered themselves as amateurs and didn't go down the pits or to the glassworks to toil over a shift of work, they believed their game to be socially and morally superior to that played 'up north', by men who still laboured above or below the ground but who earned a little extra payment for participating. Throughout the next hundred years and more, the mystique and mistakenly perceived ethos surrounding the word 'amateur' allowed rugby union's governing body, and its many members, to capture the higher moral ground and imagined social superiority over rugby league; despite the fact that many of their leading players worldwide enjoyed regular payment for playing, or received jobs and gifts in lieu of handling any filthy lucre. That moral high ground was shattered when professionalism finally became open and rampant within rugby union at all levels of the game in the Nineties and the code's leading players were, ironically, able to earn far higher wages than their counterparts in the once reviled sport of rugby league. The distinction between the two had gone but how I wish - for those of us who can enjoy both codes of rugby, can appreciate the virtues and attractions of what are essentially two different games and can enjoy the camaraderie and friendships off the field in clubhouses of both codes - that the all inclusive word 'rugby' was no longer used by some in a pathetic attempt to claim union as the pure, unadulterated version. Let us read of the Rugby Union World Cup and the Rugby League World Cup and be generous in our acknowledgement of any success. Let us acknowledge the Rugby Union Sevens in the Olympic Games and admire the perseverance of the fifteen-a-side code's governing body in its efforts to secure inclusion. And let us refer to rugby union or rugby league correspondents in our newspapers or over the airwaves. Let us acknowledge the two games for what they both are and not for what some, fancifully, perceive them to be.

No matter what the extent of the media coverage or bias there might be for a sport, whatever its financial well-being, geographical expansion and spectator interest worldwide and the numbers playing, the intrinsic qualities remain the same; enjoyment for both the player and the spectator - the entertainment factor. In Australia and Ireland, Aussie Rules and Gaelic football are hugely popular and can regularly attract eighty thousand-plus crowds, especially in Melbourne and Dublin. Attempts to expand the two codes beyond those boundaries have, however, proved difficult but that lack of expansion is not due to them being any less attractive to competitors or their passionate supporters.

Rather, perhaps, it is down to aspects of their history, their financial clout in times past or even inertia on the part of a once too complacent governing body. In such respects, rugby league has suffered since the break from its parental body in 1895 but, despite the current and hopefully temporary harsh economic climate worldwide, I sense that the game has matured considerably in its approach to expansion, is now on a secure financial footing and is continuing to provide the memories and even heartache to an ever-increasing number of fans and players, as it has done for me.

The shout of, 'gerrem onside' piercing the Norfolk countryside from a small band of spectators standing on the touchline at a South Norfolk Saints versus Ipswich Rhinos amateur match, the sight of a dozen or more barefooted seven and eight-year-old kids playing touch rugby in a jungle clearing in Papua New Guinea and the joy in the sound of a Yorkshire marching band, accompanied by a couple of hundred great Britain supporters singing to the tune of 'Colonel Bogey', making its way to the Lang Park ground in Brisbane ahead of the third and deciding Ashes Test Match in 1992, will always be treasured. Such memories illustrate the unifying effects of a sport like rugby league and the camaraderie and humour which is always there at any match, be it an amateur clash in a public park or a Challenge Cup Final at Wembley Stadium. Or even at the end of a gripping World Cup Final in Brisbane in 2008 when, having watched the odds-on favourites, Australia, being defeated by a gallant New Zealand side and observed the stunned silence of the Kangaroos fans, the five thousand-plus British supporters at the match rose from their seats and, with huge smiles on their faces, all burst into song with a chorus or two of, 'Always look on the bright side of life.' Though a sport invariably arouses the strongest passions in many of its partisans, including me, it is to be enjoyed as a pastime which can, at times, and often when you least expect it, fill you with pride, happiness and despair - often all in one afternoon! Whether as a player, spectator, coach or commentator, rugby has given me such emotions.

To prepare and then watch my Cowley School teams defeat the country's best in England and Wales in major schools rugby union sevens tournaments at Rosslyn Park, Oxford and Llanelli; to help guide a school team to victory in every match on a tour of Australia; to visit the dressing room after your school has just won the British Colleges rugby league Cup Final; or even to gather a crowd of crying, upset eleven-year-olds around you for a comforting word after a defeat, can be so satisfying and uplifting. To travel to Wembley and stand on the terraces wearing a flat cap and scarf in a pathetic attempt not to be recognised while watching my son Gary play for the St Helens under-11s schools rugby league team in a curtain-raiser to the final or later, again hopefully incognito, watch him tackle the All Blacks touring team in a North of England RU Select side at Anfield, Liverpool, can be so harsh on the nerves. More than I have ever experienced in my playing or commentating career at Wembley, Twickenham or the Sydney Cricket Ground. To see my daughter Susan, clad in a red and white scarf and sporting a huge rosette, rushing off to catch the coach for a trip to Wembley and a Cup Final involving St Helens filled me with the same pride I had when I too, as a young lad and a supporter, made the exact journey in similar colours and with equal hopes of glory.

The thrills and the drama experienced as both a BBC radio and TV commentator when covering some of the most defining moments of the game, both at home and abroad, are now part of the code's rich history. On the pitch, I still treasure the opportunity of being able to describe on television, Great Britain loose forward Mike Gregory's thrilling seventy-five yard, try scoring and match clinching dash down the middle of the pitch in Great Britain's 26-12 win over Australia, in the Third Ashes Test of 1998 in Sydney. And I will always feel a part of two of the most dramatic and groundbreaking matches ever played in the history of both codes when, in 1996, I held the Corporation's microphone at Maine Road, Manchester, while the cameras tracked the astonishing sight of them coming together when Bath met Wigan, initially under league rules. Even more upheavals were caused in the changing relationship between the two games when, some weeks later, I and BBC TV's rugby union commentator Nigel Starmer-Smith, shared the duties in the return fixture at Twickenham under fifteen-a-side rules. What an experience for someone like me to commentate for the cameras after being banned on three occasions from taking any part in rugby union by the very men who were opening the doors of Twickenham Stadium. It was in 1995 when, as rugby league correspondent for the *Today* newspaper, I sat in possibly the most important meeting in the history of rugby league since that held at the George Hotel, Huddersfield, and attended by the representatives of the twenty-one clubs which broke away from the Rugby Football Union, exactly a hundred years earlier. It was at that tense media conference where Maurice Lindsay, the RFL's chief executive, announced to a stunned sporting world that Rupert Murdoch and News Corporation were to inject a staggering eighty-seven million pound package into the game and that a new era of summer rugby and Super League would follow within twelve months.

Memorable matches and history making occasions all, but oh, the talented players and exciting personalities I have played with and against, or on whose heroic deeds I have commentated. The likes of my contemporaries Alex

Murphy, Tom van Vollenhoven, Dick Huddart, Vince Karalius, Eric Ashton, Billy Boston, Mick Sullivan, Brian McTigue, Neil Fox, Derek Turner, Roger Millward, Mal Reilly, Lewis Jones, Brian Bevan, Alan Hardisty, Cliff Watson, John Whiteley, Ike Southward and so many others make me feel that I played in a 'golden age', but I know only too well that there were players who went before who were surely their equals and that in recent decades the likes of Martin Offiah, Ellery Hanley, Jonathan Davies, Shaun Edwards, Garry Schofield, Gary Connolly, Kevin Ward, Chris Joynt, Keiron Cunningham, Jamie Peacock, Adrian Morley, Jason Robinson, Andy Farrell and company stand to challenge them on the pedestal of fame. Sadly, thanks to the development and success of summer rugby in Britain and the emergence and importance of international rugby league to the individual nations of England, Wales, Scotland and Ireland, no longer will their successors have the chance to come together as a British RL Lions tour party. As a composite, they will not have the opportunity to challenge the might of Australia in an Ashes Test series Down Under or against the Kiwis Down Under. The demise of the Lions tours is a huge loss to the game and one which denies the leading players in Britain the right to perform on what once was the biggest stage in rugby league.

My life in rugby has been a full and satisfying one and I do believe that by maintaining a keen interest in union, alongside my confessed obsession for league, it has enabled me to appreciate the attractions of both - and to judge the integrity of the actions of one by noting the honesty of the other.

Though rightly still rivals, both codes have, by the linking up of clubs or mergers at both professional and amateur level, and by the easy and regular freedom of movement of players between the two games, gained a better insight and understanding of each others reason for being and what they have to offer to young and old. In common with all other team sports, rugby league is experiencing difficulty in raising the level of interest at the turnstiles of clubs in the lower leagues but the overall standard of the game is high in Britain, while Super League is currently providing some of the most competitive matches in its short fifteen-year existence.

Despite being battered and bruised by the words and deeds of powerful men within the Rugby Football Union as it fought for its very life in the early years after the 'great split', plundered and outlawed throughout France in wartime and vilified and scorned in a media often all too hostile to it for daring to pay players, rugby league has not only survived but thrived and should have no fears for its future. The players are respected widely for their strength, fitness, athleticism, discipline, sportsmanship, courage and skill and the game is acknowledged as being one of the most exciting and competitive of team sports. It is watched and enjoyed by an ever increasing number of families and supporters who can wear their favourites' colours without fear of being confined and separated from their opponents' fans on the terraces, behind barriers or ranks of policemen. The 'breakaway' game is now an attraction in its own right for, as Simon Barnes, *The Times* sports columnist insists: 'The great charm of rugby league is that every now and then comes that moment of revelation. Rugby league operates on a relentless rhythm, but every now and then that rhythm is dramatically broken and the game is, in an instant, operating on a completely different pattern. It's a game that explodes.'

So let us put aside any conspiracy theories as to why our sport often fails to attract its just deserts in the written media, forget the real or imagined slights paid to it over the past hundred years and more and ignore the bigots within both games who still command attention for their outspoken, mistaken and misguided views. Let us shout the virtues of rugby league from the rooftops and encourage others to see just what enjoyment and entertainment it has to offer for those who play or watch it. But let us always remember that the game has no god-given right to prosper and that its rightful position in any hierarchy of sport will only come about by sheer hard work and devotion.

BIBLIOGRAPHY

Billy Boston, Rugby League Footballer by Robert Gate - London League Publications Ltd; *Centenary History of the Rugby Football Union* by U.A. Titley & Ross McWhirter - RFU Publishing; *Code 13* (Booklet) by Trevor Delaney; *Destination Wembley: The History of the Rugby League Challenge Cup* by Graham Morris - Vertical Editions; *Saints v Wigan. Derby Matches* by Robert Gate - Smiths Books (Wigan) Ltd; *Saints in their Glory. The History of the St Helens Rugby League Club 1874-1939* by Alex Service; *The March of the Saints. St Helens Rugby League Club.1945-1985* by Alex Service; *The British Rugby League Records Book* by Graham Williams, Peter Lush, Dave Farrar - London League Publications Ltd; *Tries in the Valleys: A History of Rugby League in Wales* by Peter Lush & Dave Farrar - London League Publications Ltd; *Rugby's Class War: Bans, boot money and parliamentary battles* by David Hinchliffe MP - London League Publications Ltd.